INDOOR GARDENING

Learning How to Grow Fruits, Vegetables and Herbs for Beginners

By Tom Gordon

© Copyright 2020 - All rights reserved.

The content contained within this book may not be reproduced, duplicated or transmitted without direct written permission from the author or the publisher.

Under no circumstances will any blame or legal responsibility be held against the publisher, or author, for any damages, reparation, or monetary loss due to the information contained within this book. Either directly or indirectly.

Legal Notice:

This book is copyright protected. This book is only for personal use. You cannot amend, distribute, sell, use, quote or paraphrase any part, or the content within this book, without the consent of the author or publisher.

Disclaimer Notice:

Please note the information contained within this document is for educational and entertainment purposes only. All effort has been executed to present accurate, up to date, and reliable, complete information. No warranties of any kind are declared or implied. Readers acknowledge that the author is not engaging in the rendering of legal, financial, medical or professional advice. The content within this book has been derived from various sources. Please consult a licensed professional before attempting any techniques outlined in this book.

INDOOR GARDENING

By reading this document, the reader agrees that under no circumstances is the author responsible for any losses, direct or indirect, which are incurred as a result of the use of information contained within this document, including, but not limited to, — errors, omissions, or inaccuracies.

INDOOR GARDENING

Table of Contents

Introduction 5

Chapter One - Where To Grow Your Garden Indoors 10

Chapter Two - Getting Started Gardening 26

Chapter Three - The Operation Cycle Of An Indoor Garden 47

Chapter Four - Growing Beautiful Fruits 66

Chapter Five - Cultivating Delicious Vegetables 93

Chapter Six - Planting Healthy Herbs 110

Chapter Seven - Common Mistakes And How To Avoid Them 129

Final Words 141

INDOOR GARDENING

INTRODUCTION

INDOOR GARDENING

More and more people are getting into gardening every day. With the current focus on living green and eco-friendly lifestyles, gardening has become cool again. Some people enjoy doing their part to help the environment, others enjoy the feeling of taking care of a living organism, and others simply want to grow their own fruits, vegetables, and herbs. There are only a few things in this life as satisfying as a home-cooked meal with fresh ingredients you grew yourself. Plus, when you grow yourself you can be sure that no harmful chemicals have slipped into your meals.

When most people hear the word gardening, they think of a plot of land with a little farm or the corner of a backyard that has been converted into a vegetable patch. Gardening seems to go hand in hand with the outdoors. They have been traditionally paired together, a staple of many North American paintings and stories. But here in the 21st century, it can take a lot of work to get access to land for gardening. Some cities have communal gardens where you can rent a space but this option doesn't fit everyone. With more people living in apartment buildings than ever before, we find the need to expand how we consider gardening. It is time to embrace the indoor garden.

If you're reading this introduction, then there's a good chance that you are ready to start your indoor garden, but you just don't know how yet. Don't worry, this book will cover everything you need to get set up and start growing your own fruits and vegetables. But there is also the possibility that you haven't decided if indoor gardening is right for you yet. This is understandable, as there are just as many cons to indoor gardening as there are pros. Let's take a look at the good and the bad of indoor gardening so you can weigh both sides and decide if it is right for you.

Let's begin with the pros. Indoor gardening allows more people to take part and join the gardening wave that is sweeping through the culture. Because of a lack of access to ground to plant a garden outdoors, indoor gardening may be a necessity for those that want to garden. But that necessity also allows for a lot of flexibility. Planting in the ground, you know exactly where your plants need to go. But an indoor garden can be done on a bookshelf, a dedicated space for a hydroponic setup, or even in hanging baskets around the living room. In this manner, indoor gardening actually allows for quite a variety of approaches.

You are also able to fully take control of the environment in which your garden is raised. From setting up lights to provide heat, establishing fans to keep the air fresh, and arranging plenty of water, you are able to fine-tune your garden in much greater depth when it is indoors. If you have an outdoor garden that needs a lot of light, then an overcast day can do serious harm to your plants. But an indoor garden uses electric lights to simulate the sun, and that means it doesn't matter if it is sunny, overcast or raining, your plants are always under your control. This level of control, when respected and utilized with intention, also means you can avoid issues with pests and disease much easier than you could with an outdoor garden. However, that will lead us into our first con as well.

Just because it is easier to avoid pests and disease when gardening indoors doesn't mean that they aren't still an issue. In fact, when pests take to an indoor garden, it can be even harder to repel them than if they were outdoors. Predatory insects seem even less appealing when you're looking at releasing them into your living room, after all! If you are going to garden indoors, then you need to make sure you keep your garden clean and tidy, well-fed, and properly protected. All of this equals more chores around the house on a daily basis. This means time and energy have to be committed to the garden's upkeep, time and energy that you may not feel compelled to give after a long day at work.

Other problems that indoor gardens face are a bit cuter. If you have children or pets, then you could run into problems with keeping your garden safe. Children have a tendency to break just about everything they get their hands on, and pets, such as cats, may use your garden as a litter box or even get sick (and possibly die) from chewing on the plants you are growing. What this means is that if you have children or pets, then you need to consider the security of your garden much more deeply than you would if it were outdoors.

While an indoor garden offers control over the environmental factors at play, these can prove to be difficult to keep in check when put in practice. Making sure that the temperature and lighting your plants need is correct may take up more time than you imagine. This is true even when these elements are automated. Automating your garden isn't an excuse to ignore your garden. The biggest con yet though, is that even if you take care of all of these, even if you make sure to battle pests and keep the environment in check, you may still find that your plants just aren't as tasty as those grown outdoors. Making sure you look after everything properly should keep this from being too big an issue, but many growers find they can taste the difference between an indoor or an outdoor tomato.

Those are the pros and cons. You may notice that many of the cons are only negatives when they are compared with outdoor gardening. If you don't have the option to choose between indoor and outdoor, then that con list should look quite a bit smaller. The fact of the matter is that an indoor garden is absolutely more fun and enjoyable than having no garden at all. So if you are ready to start raising delicious fruits, vegetables, and herbs in your home, then flip the page to get started!

CHAPTER ONE

WHERE TO GROW YOUR GARDEN INDOORS

When it comes to growing a garden indoors, the first step is to prepare the space necessary for your growing operation. You may only want a couple of plants hanging up in your living room, or you might want to dedicate a room of your apartment to act as your personal greenhouse. Regardless of which you choose, it is important to consider the space itself. Will your plants get enough sun there, or will you need to invest in lights? Will you have access to all of your plants in this design, or are there some you won't be able to reach? Are the temperature and humidity going to be manageable there?

Starting with these questions first is important as it allows you to get a good sense of your growing operation before you even spend a dollar. Questions about sunlight and humidity might be best answered when you know what kinds of fruits and vegetables you want to plant rather than just guessing the answers. If you already

INDOOR GARDENING

know what you want to plant, then you can follow the directions for the best humidity and hours of daylight they'll need. If you aren't fully sure what you want to plant, you don't need to worry. The advice covered in this chapter will ensure that you pick the best possible spot for your garden.

Working with Available Space

You don't need to go out and rent a new apartment or greenhouse just to have an indoor garden. Chances are you have plenty of space available to you right this second if you use it properly. Bookcases, windowsills, hanging plants, you can fit a whole vegetable garden into your living room with a little bit of creativity. Of course, if you want to go big, then we're going to address that as well. But it is important to keep in mind that it really doesn't take up a lot of space to start gardening. You could even spread your garden out between rooms if you had to: keep your tomatoes in the living room while your lettuce is in the bedroom. The only thing stopping you is the limits of your imagination. In this section, we are going to make the assumption that you're looking to do a little bigger setup than this, enough that you will need to consider the space more objectively. However, keep in mind that many of the tips for larger growing operations are equally applicable to smaller ones as well.

When it comes to picking the right space for your garden, it is important to consider how much sunlight the room gets and how much control you have over both the humidity and the temperature of the space. These three points will be discussed in more detail in a moment, but you should keep them in mind when deciding what location to use. If you find that you are going to need equipment such as a dehumidifier or grow lamps, then you need to dedicate a larger space to the grow than if you can rely on the natural features of the space. It can be a good idea to sketch out the area you are looking to grow and to take notes on all of these different elements. When you have them all down on paper in front of you, you may find that the space isn't as ideal as you first thought.

Regardless of where you choose, you are going to want to make sure it can be properly set up to maintain your plants with minimal exposure to the risk of disease and infestation. Some gardeners like to set up their plants behind security measures such as a zippered airlock to help minimize risk. This is especially true for those that choose to grow using a hydroponic method, though we will be focusing our attention on soil-grown plants. Since this is the case, our best bet in reducing infection is to ensure that we use an area with proper flooring and good ventilation to promote healthy airflow.

Flooring may seem like an odd choice to focus on when you consider that our plants will be in pots, and therefore not touching the floor. There are two reasons that we want to keep flooring in mind. The first is the reduction of risk and this means that you should avoid setting up your garden in a carpeted space. For one, carpets can get damaged and even begin to grow mold due to spills during watering. Carpets also catch and hold onto a lot of bacteria and germs, and this is very unhealthy for your plants. Mold is going to be something you need to watch out for in general when it comes to your plants; for example, part of maintaining your garden is removing dead plant matter that can then rot and mold and spread disease. It is a lot harder to tell that there is a problem with your carpet than it is to remove fallen plant matter. Some people dislike setting up their gardens in a room with a wooden floor because watering can cause damage to it as well. However, you can minimize this risk by setting up a tarp for your plants to rest on. Just make sure the tarp can easily be cleaned, and you have a way to remove any spilled water. The biggest recommendations for flooring are slate, linoleum or ceramic, though we don't always have the option to choose one of these.

Airflow is vital to your plants. You probably know that your plants can drown when overwatered. It might sound a little weird to hear, but did you know that your plants can suffocate, too? When you're in a stuffy room, you begin to overheat and lose your breath, right? This can happen to your plants as well. Their leaves will let go of moisture, almost like they were sweating. A little bit of this is perfectly normal; in fact, it is what allows your plants to gather more water from the soil. But if they get too hot, too stuffy, then they can't breathe the air anymore and they begin to wilt and die. This needs to be considered when choosing your growing space. You might be able to fit a few plants and the necessary lights into that broom closet of yours, but the lack of airflow could leave you with a bunch of dead plants. You need to either have a natural airflow that they can benefit from or provide them with fans to keep the air circulating.

A healthy circulation of air does more than just keep your plants alive, though. Proper ventilation and airflow will see a reduction in harmful bacteria and mold that can cause disease; it will also help to make it harder for pests to take up home on your plants. Due to the small

INDOOR GARDENING

size of many garden pests, the airflow will make it difficult for them to properly control their bodies to land on your plants. That same breeze that makes it harder for pests to land can help your plants in their pollination phase, though chances are you won't have to worry about this since you're focusing on fruits, vegetables, and herbs. What's more important than the assistance with pollination is the fact that a decent breeze will strengthen your plants. Branches will grow stronger due to the breeze, and this will promote root growth and lead to better harvests. Plants need CO_2 in the air in order to best grow. When in a room with stale air, they will suck up all the CO_2 and then start to suffocate. Healthy airflow will bring plenty of fresh CO_2 and oxygen into your grow space so that you can have healthy, high yielding plants. Plus, airflow will help in keeping the temperature and humidity levels in check. So when you are planning your space, pay attention to the way that the air moves through the area. If it doesn't, then you are going to have to invest in some fans and these will take up space, so it is best to plan around them early.

Finally, we will be talking about sunlight more in depth in a moment but it needs to be considered here as well. Plants need light; it is pretty much a rule of thumb with all plants unless you are purposefully growing something with very unusual needs. When considering the space, pay attention to the sunlight it will get. Growing indoors often means you can't rely purely on sunlight but rather need to purchase grow lights. Like all equipment, these take up space that should be planned for. Grow lights also eat up electricity and this means a monetary cost is associated with them. Your best option is likely to use a combination of sunlight and electric illumination. Basically, this means that you find out how much sun the space gets and then use the lights to give your plants the extra boost they need. For example, tomatoes need at least eight hours of light. If you can rely on the sunlight for six hours of the day then you only need to prove another two or three hours of light through your gear. Gardening indoors often requires this sort of flexibility to ensure a delicious harvest.

Using Natural Sunlight

When we garden outdoors, we obviously trust the sun to provide our plants with everything they need. There may be overcast or rainy days that cause issues, but we typically don't set up lights to compensate for these. We give our trust over completely to the natural order of things. However, when it comes to indoor gardening, this becomes much trickier. Our access to the sun is dependent on windows, doorways, and the like. We can still make use of the sun but it is going to take more consideration than simply planting in the backyard and letting nature take its course. In order to best make use of our glowing orange globe, let's take a moment to consider how it moves in relation to your gardening space.

INDOOR GARDENING

The first thing to remember is that the sun rises in the east and sets in the west. Since this happens every single day, we can use this to set up an experiment to see how much sun we can capture indoors. But in order to do this, you need to first figure out which direction your apartment or house is facing. One way to do this is to grab a compass and see which direction each wall is in. If you don't have a compass, don't worry, you can do this from the comfort of your computer chair. Go to maps.google.com and input your address. Click on the satellite view button and you'll see that the view includes a compass in the corner. You can use this to see exactly which way everything is facing and use this to help you determine the best location for your garden to get plenty of sun. But hold up, there's one more important step.

If you live in the Northern Hemisphere, then the winter sun will rise in the southeast, head more south, and then set in the southwest. This leaves the sun on the south side throughout the day. The summer sun will rise in the northeast and travel over to the northwest, leaving it more on the north side of the house throughout the day. Knowing this, you can judge whether you want to plant facing the north or the south. So now we know how the sun travels and which section of your dwelling it is going to be at, but this still doesn't fully capture everything you need. There is one last step that you need to consider: the environment around you.

Take a look out of the windows in the grow space you are considering. If you live in the city, you may have buildings that are blocking out part of the sun's path; if you dwell in the country, then you may have trees and foliage that cast shade. Depending on how they block the sun's path, these could cause major issues. As an example, if you have a building that stops sunlight from getting to your plants for two hours of the day, then this can certainly be harmful to your plants. Just like you and I need our sleep, and our bodies tend to set their rhythms based on how much light is around us, so too do plants. When they lose the light for those hours, they will think it is time to sleep. This will lead to a rude awakening when they are suddenly hit with a strong burst of sunlight two hours later. It may seem silly to worry about the sleep patterns of your plants, but this affects them adversely and leads to health complications and a reduction in yield.

By taking the time to research the sun's relationship with your grow space, you will be able to identify possible issues such as this ahead of time. One solution to this particular problem would be to invest in some grow lights and an automatic timer. You can set the timer so the lights come on fifteen minutes before the sun disappears behind the obstruction, and turn off fifteen minutes after it peeks back out. As the arc of the sun changes throughout the year, it is useful to keep track of what it is doing so that you can adjust the required time as necessary. By setting it up to have a fifteen minute window of overlap, you create a safety buffer to ensure that your plants always get the light they need to stay healthy and strong.

Thinking about Temperature and Humidity Control

The final piece that you need to consider in this planning stage is that of the temperature and the humidity of the grow space. Different plants require different temperatures and humidity levels, which means that you may need to consider a second grow space if you are looking to produce something completely out of sync with the majority of your garden.

That said, you can almost certainly bet that whichever space you pick will need to have more humidity added to it. Plants just love the stuff. Remember how we

INDOOR GARDENING

mentioned that plants breathe? The pores from which they breathe lose moisture when the air around them is dry. This can leave the plants shriveled up and dead very quickly. A good rule of thumb when it comes to plants is the thicker the plant's leaves are, the less humidity it will require. The humidity for an indoor vegetable garden should be around the 40%-50% range. If you don't know the humidity of your grow space, you can purchase a hygrometer at most drugstores. These handy little devices will let you monitor indoor humidity.

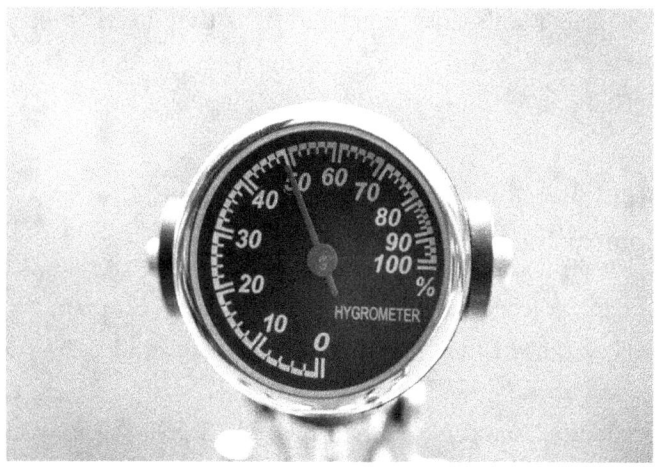

Hygrometer in hand, check the grow space throughout the day. While going in and just getting a single rating may do the trick, it is always best to have an idea of how the space changes throughout the day. The space will probably need to have humidity added to it, which you can do by setting up a humidifier. But don't forget, every new piece of equipment you need to add to your garden will require space. It is important to bear that in mind so that you always reach each and every plant. Cutting off access to a plant almost guarantees that you'll neglect to give it the care it needs. With the new humidifier, you can set a timer to keep the humidity in check at all times, thanks to the notes you took with the hygrometer.

A vast majority of the vegetables you are likely to grow will require a temperature of 65-75F. Plants won't immediately die if they are slightly off from their preferred temperature. You can most likely keep alive one that wants 65F while growing those that want 75F, but the yield will reflect this.

Go out and grab yourself an indoor thermometer. There are some that can be programmed to record the temperature at set intervals; such an instrument could be a worthwhile investment. As with the humidity, you want to keep track of the temperature of your chosen space throughout the day. It is obviously going to fluctuate greatly as the day changes to night. A top-range thermometer will let you see if you need to add heaters or fans to adjust the temperature of the room. You will want to have a fan going, so remember to take the temperature both with and without that being active. If you have yet to get the fan, then you can adjust these numbers later on. The important thing is to keep track of them so that you always know exactly what is happening with your plants. This level of attention may seem unnecessary, but your garden's yield will show you why it pays to treat your plants well.

INDOOR GARDENING

Chapter Summary

- With a little creativity, you can grow vegetables all around your house. Bookshelves, window ledges, and hanging pots are all options available for would-be gardeners short on space!

- It is likely though that you will want to set aside a designated space for your garden. This will make it easier to maintain proper temperature, humidity, and light control. It will also reduce the risk of plants getting infected by harmful bacteria.

- Some indoor gardeners like to set aside a room for their plants or raise them in tents. That's a good idea; it reduces the chance of infection and keeps them safe.

- You want to ensure that your grow space is ventilated and that it has a decent airflow, either naturally or by purchasing a fan. This will help to reduce the risk of infestation and promote healthy growth. It will also prevent your plants from suffocating!

- Your growing space should not be on a carpeted floor. Carpets capture lots of bacteria and they can easily be water damaged. A wooden surface is all right if you can put down a tarp first, but the best options are slate, linoleum, or ceramic flooring.

INDOOR GARDENING

- Even if you're able to make use of natural sunlight to light your plants, the chances are good that you will still need to purchase a few grow lights. Always remember to calculate space for equipment as well as for plants. You want to be able to reach all your plants to give them proper care.

- Find out which direction your apartment or house faces to decide where you can expect sunlight to come from throughout the year.

- Natural sunlight is great for your plants, but there are many things that can obstruct its pathway to your garden. Learning how much sun your room is getting is important, as you may need to supplement natural lighting with artificial lighting so that your plants get enough to survive.

- Because of the way their pores work, plants need to have moisture in the air. Without it, they begin to suffocate and die. You want the humidity in your grow space to rest around 40%-50%. There is a good chance that you will need to use a humidifier for this.

- Most vegetables also want a temperature between 65-75F. Use a thermometer to track the temperature of your space to get a sense of how much you need to raise or lower the temperature. Don't forget that you will be using a fan in the area, as well as lights.

INDOOR GARDENING

In the next chapter, you will learn how to choose the right container for your plants to live and grow. You'll also learn more about the different materials and tools you'll need to look after your vegetable or fruit garden. From lights to fans, soil to shears, you'll have everything you need to start and care for your personal indoor garden.

CHAPTER TWO

GETTING STARTED GARDENING

Now that you have chosen a space for your garden, it is time to start gathering all of the necessary materials and putting them together. We'll talk about the tools discussed in the last chapter, the fans and humidifiers. However, we'll primarily be talking about the containers which home our plants, the growing medium that they live in, and the various tools that we use to look after them and keep them healthy.

By the end of this chapter, you should be able to put together a shopping list for all the items you need to look after your garden. In creating this list, it is worthwhile to note that we are not looking at the supplies necessary for growing a hydroponic garden. While hydroponic gardens function perfectly well indoors, they have an entirely different set of needs than the plants we are raising in this garden. We're getting our hands dirty in the soil just like people used to!

Picking the Right Container for Your Plants

There are two steps to picking the perfect container for your plants. The first is to consider the size of container that type of plant needs. We'll first take a quick look at the different sizes and what they are used to grow. But the other step is to consider the material that the container is made out of. Once you have figured out what is right for your needs, there will still be one last step you should consider when making your list.

Pots come in all different sizes. At the lower end are tiny 10-inch pots. On the higher end are your 30-inch ones or 3 gallons on the small end and 30 gallons on the high. You also have 14, 16, 18 and 24 inch pots which are typically used. If you go after unique shapes and designs, then you may end up with oddly shaped pots that don't line up with these. By focusing our attention on these sizes, you will be able to see the difference between them

INDOOR GARDENING

and use that knowledge to make an educated guess on what you can grow in any weird pots you end up with. Trust me, once you get gardening, people have a tendency to give you pots as gifts.

10-inch: In a pot as small as this, you can only grow a herb like mint or sage. Or you could grow a single strawberry or head of leaf lettuce. You could go crazy and grow four turnips or a dozen French carrots but that's pretty much it.

14-inch: One cabbage, four peas, a single collard. You can go crazy here and plant ten carrots, regular-sized ones instead of the smaller French rounds. You could probably get away with three heads of leaf lettuce. Four if you're careful.

16-inch: Now you can really get away with growing some great vegetables. You can fit everything from before but now in greater quantity. However, this is still too small for many vegetables.

18-inch: There's a good chance that you'll be looking at pots of this size or higher for your garden. This is because one of these can house an eggplant, a pepper, a cauliflower, a tomato bush, or broccoli. Still, it can only fit one of those because they're bigger plants.

24-inch: You can grow cucumbers, blackberries, raspberries, vining tomatoes, squash, or even a fig tree with a 24-inch pot. Again, you'll only be growing one of these per pot.

30-inch: Chances are you'll only use a 30-inch container if you want to grow really large and heavy plants such as cherry trees, sweet corn, pumpkins, or rhubarb.

Using this guide to plan out what pots you need, you should be able to settle on some sizes now. So let's turn our attention over to the material. The most popular choices are between plastic, wood, terracotta, or ceramic. Each of these has its pros and cons. However, you need to make sure that whatever kind you go with has built-in drainage so that you don't drown your plants.

Right off, you should probably avoid wooden pots. While these are popular for many growers, they do have their drawbacks. For one, they will slowly break apart over time. They also can rot from water damage, which isn't ideal when you consider how much plants enjoy their water. Ceramic is a better choice than wood and often looks quite beautiful and brightly colored. They're great for indoor plants but they are one of the most expensive options.

If you are concerned about price, then terracotta or plastic might prove more affordable than ceramic. Plastic containers are very light, which makes it easier to move your plants. However, this can lead to issues if you are looking to grow heavy plants. Plastic tends to be the

INDOOR GARDENING

cheapest to purchase, though they are prone to breaking down just as much, if not more, than wooden pots. Terracotta, on the other hand, is cheaper than ceramic but more expensive than plastic. It is also much heavier than plastic. Terracotta pots have a tendency to dry quicker than the other kinds, so, if you use them, you will need to water your plants more often. Of course, if you are growing some herbs that enjoy dryer climes, then this can be a blessing.

Regardless of which you go with, you can expect each category to sell at a range of prices depending on how fancy the pot is. You can easily spend a couple of hundred dollars on pots that could be bought for $20 in a cheaper design. Your plant will enjoy a boring container just as much as they do a pretty one, so this is all about what you want rather than what the plant needs.

There is one more thing about containers that should be addressed. It is a smart idea to purchase some smaller ones which you can use for planting seeds. When you plant a seed, you do so in a smaller container, and then move it to its larger home when it has grown to a healthy size. Having some smaller containers around is always a good idea. Just as you'll end up being given pots as a gift, people also will start giving you seeds. You never know when you might have a new vegetable joining your garden.

INDOOR GARDENING

Picking the Perfect Soil

There are all sorts of different kits out there with marketing that tells you exactly why you should use their soil and only their soil. This can make it seem like choosing the right type is a stressful experience. The truth of the matter is it doesn't have to be stressful at all. If you care about the taste of your vegetables, then you must use an organic potting mix. You can go to any gardening store and say, "I'm looking for an organic potting mix for use in growing vegetables in containers," and they will set you up fine. Or, as we'll discuss here, you can make your own if you are feeling crafty.

Buying the potting soil from the store will ensure that you have exactly what your plants crave but it can end up costing you a pretty penny. Making your own will save you this penny and it really isn't that hard. An excellent homemade soil is composed of a growing medium, a material to keep in moisture, and another to allow for the plant to be drained.

Before we get started at making our own soil, it is important to consider fertilizing that soil. When you buy a pre-made mix from the store, it will start out with plenty of nutrients. However, your plants are going to suck up those nutrients so that they can grow. Since your plants continue to need these nutrients, adding fertilizer to the soil is done in order to keep it. If you choose to make your own potting mix then you should also add a little bit of fertilizer at the beginning and then, same with the pre-bought mix, add more to it on a regular schedule. A couple of ways of adding fertilizer are to add some limestone to your homemade soil at the beginning and to top-dress the plants with healthy compost, such as mushroom compost. Of course, there are also many kinds of fertilizer that you can find at your local garden store. Now let's take a look at those recipes.

If you want to create a potting soil that is designed to function the same way that store- bought potting soil does, then you want to take a large pot and add in your three ingredients. For a growing medium you can use the kind of garden soil you would find at any hardware store. These mediums should already be treated to ensure that they are free of disease or weeds. Of course, you could always just go out and scoop up some soil yourself, but this is almost certainly guaranteed to be a bad idea. In order to ensure that moisture, and therefore more nutrients, are retained in your mix, you should add in peat moss. Finally, you want to make sure your mix won't drown your plants, and this means adding a drainage material such as vermiculite, sand, or perlite. Take these three ingredients and mix them, keeping the proportions equal. You want your potting mix to be loose when you stir but to clump up when you squeeze it in your hands.

For some people, this mix is not organic enough. Another recipe for homemade potting mix, this time favored by organic growers, is to mix garden soil and compost. You can actually go to the store and purchase compost for this reason, or you can make your own. The best compost for growing vegetables comes from a mixture of vegetable scraps or peelings, bread, eggshells, pieces of fruit, or coffee grounds. Whatever you do, make sure you don't include any animal products like meat or fat or even daily products. You want the compost to be half green, half brown (such as using dried leaves or scraps of cardboard). Mix one-half soil, one-half compost, and add sand to the mix to allow for drainage.

Whether you use store-bought or you make your own, it's important to give your plants what they need.

Lights, Fans, Humidifiers

INDOOR GARDENING

We talked about the need for lights, fans, and humidifiers in the last chapter, so we will only briefly touch on them here so that you can add them to your shopping list as needed. As with everything, there is quite a range of prices that you can find yourself paying for this equipment. Truthfully, though, don't think that more money equals better plants. It is almost always a smarter choice to start small and get the more expensive gear down the road as you better understand what you are doing.

Fans and humidifiers are very easy to understand. You want a humidifier that will give you the 40-50% levels you need, and you want a fan that will blow air. This means pretty much any humidifier or fan will do the trick. Now, if you want to get a little fancier, you can purchase models that regulate themselves. A humidifier that knows when to turn off and on by reading the room can save you having to finetune the schedule of garden maintenance. However, this can still be done with cheaper models by purchasing a timer. By using a timer, you can set your cheap fan or humidifier to turn off and on based on the schedule you built using the information you collected in the previous chapter. You can also use a timer for your grow lights, which we'll turn our attention to now.

Although the lights in your home might make the room plenty bright for you, your plants are far more discriminating when it comes to the light they crave.

INDOOR GARDENING

Plants use light to go through a process called photosynthesis, and the lights in your home just won't do the trick to trigger this. That means purchasing lights especially designed for plants. What separates regular lights from plant lights is the spectrum of light that they produce. Go to a site like Amazon and open up the product page for the first light you can find. You'll notice that the description includes numbers with a K afterward such as 3000K. This tells you how warm or how cold the light is. The higher the number, the colder the light. While there are quite a few plants that will grow with a cold light, if you want a proper and healthy harvest, then you will need a warmer light in the 3000K range. There are three primary kinds of lights that growers purchase for their indoor gardens. Feel free to choose the kind that is right for you, but just make sure that it is a warm light so that your plants are happy with it, and you don't need to replace it for a warmer one down the road.

Fluorescent grow lights are used quite regularly by indoor growers. The standard bulb, referred to as the T12, is often used to help provide extra light for plants near windows. However, the T12 is not overly strong, and so these lights need to be placed close to the plants in order to really provide any benefit. More appropriate for an indoor gardener is the T5 bulb. Thinner than the T12, the T5 is a more powerful light that is strong enough to care for a plant without the extra boost of natural sunlight. If you are going to go with fluorescent grow lights, then you are best served by purchasing a T5 or a similarly powerful variation thereof.

LED grow lights have become very popular lately. These lights are more expensive than the fluorescent ones, but they are designed to use only half as much electricity. This means that purchasing an LED grow light might cost you up-front, but it will save you money in the long run. They also last four to five times longer than fluorescent bulbs do, which makes those savings even more impressive. Keep in mind that if you are looking to use an LED light for your garden, then you are going to need to purchase one specifically meant for use with plants because most LED lights are simply not strong enough. But those that have been intended for plants are typically far more intense than the fluorescent bulbs are. LED lights also don't run as hot, which means that they won't make as large of an impact on your grow space's overall temperature.

HID grow lights were the most popular light for indoor gardeners before the rise of LED technology. People who were only raising one or two plants would go with fluorescent bulbs while those with many would always turn to HID. They are the most expensive of the three kinds but they also tend to be the most powerful. They don't use electricity sparingly either, so they can lead to a heavier electricity bill compared to the other kinds of light. However, they are great for growing plants like tomatoes that have a lot of foliage because the intensity allows the light to get through to the roots easier. HID lights come in high pressure sodium and metal halide varieties. High pressure sodium lights are used for the flowering phase of the plant's life, while metal halide is used during the vegetative growth period. You can get away with using just one of these types throughout the whole growth cycle, but if you decide to use both for your indoor garden, then you will need to buy two different types of fixtures rather than just swap out the bulbs between a single fixture.

While the choice of what type of light to use is entirely your own, it is this author's recommendation that you begin with a decent LED grow light. As the middle option, they will still cost more to set up than a fluorescent light does, but the longer life cycle and the reduced electricity consumption will quickly make up for this investment. LED grow lights will also allow you to produce more plants at the same time than the fluorescent bulbs will. Before you add the lights to your shopping list, let's first consider how much illumination you will need to provide.

As a rule of thumb, if you are growing a plant that produces any type of food, then it is pretty safe to assume that it will require a minimum of 30 watts of light for every square foot. However, because we are looking not just to keep the plants alive but to produce an amazing harvest, the best bet is to aim to provide 50 watts per square foot instead. To figure out how much you require, you will need a measuring tape. Measure out the grow space that you have set aside for your plants. Multiply the length by the width to get the square footage. Take this number and multiply it by 50, which is to say multiply the square footage of your grow area by the amount of wattage your plants need. This gives you the exact wattage that you need to purchase. Every light that you can buy will have the wattage listed on the package or, if you are buying online, the store page. Divide the total wattage you need by how many watts the light puts out. This number tells you exactly how many lights you need. Here's an example of the math:

A 5x5 grow area has a square footage of 25. 25 multiplied by 50 equals 1250, which means that this grow area requires 1250 watts of light. The first grow light I found shows a wattage of 185, so I will take 1250 and divide it by 185 to get 6.75. Round this up to 7. I now know exactly how many lights I need to purchase. Keep in mind, this example is using a made-up space and the first grow light I found on a quick Google search. Your space and the lights you purchase may line up to these numbers, but it is more likely that you will need to calculate your specific numbers. Once you have, you know exactly how many lights to provide for your plants and can add these to your shopping list.

Everything Else You Need

INDOOR GARDENING

Even when the big equipment has all been tackled, there will still be quite a few pieces that you will want to purchase before you start your garden. These range from hand tools to oils and soil test kits. The good news is that most of these will only cost you a couple of dollars each and can be found in pretty much any gardening or hardware store. But first, we won't be covering seeds here. If you want to grow a plant, you will need to purchase seeds or a young plant. This one should go without saying and only you know exactly what fruits and vegetables you are interested in growing. If you don't yet know, we'll be covering fruits, vegetables, and herbs in chapters four, five and six.

As your plants grow, you will find yourself needing to take care of them, and maintaining their health will mean tools. But if you want your plants to grow at all, you will need to water them. You have three options for this. The first is to get yourself a watering can and use that. While using a watering can simply makes it easier to pour the water, many people enjoy using them because they give the feeling of being a "real" gardener. You can just as easily save your money and use a measuring cup or even a simple drinking cup. Just remember to keep the gardening cup separate from those you drink from as there are times when you will want to add plant nutrients to your water that you wouldn't care to directly consume yourself! Finally, if you are looking for a more expensive but mostly hands-free approach, you can always

INDOOR GARDENING

purchase a system that automates your watering for you on a timer.

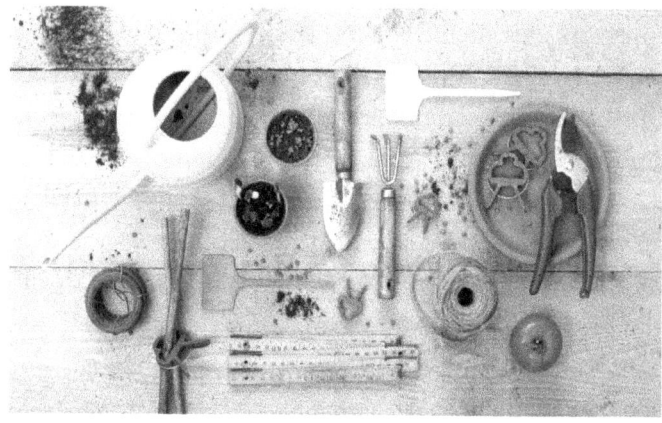

In order to trim and maintain the plants as they grow, you will want to get several types of hand tools. First up is a set of shears for pruning. You'll need to cut your plants at certain points to promote healthy growth or to remove infected limbs. You could use a set of scissors, but these may create a harsh cut, which would hurt your plant. Every time you cut your plants, they receive a shock to their system. A good set of shears will ensure that the cuts you do make as little harm as possible. You will also want to get a small rake for the soil and a trowel, though these aren't nearly as important as shears. What is as important is to get yourself a spade. You'll want to be able to dig down underneath the roots, especially when they are young, and you need to move them from their seeding pot to the larger growing pot.

INDOOR GARDENING

While you will more than likely find yourself using shears to remove unhealthy limbs, the best option available to us gardeners is to prevent infection or infestation before it happens. We already spoke about some ways of doing this earlier, but another effective way is to purchase some neem oil. Neem oil is made out of natural chemicals found from pressing vegetable oil out of the fruit and seeds of the neem herb. These chemicals are used to deter pests like mites and to strive off infectious diseases and fungi. You can purchase it at pretty much any gardening center, and it should be applied to your plants once every week. Since it is most cost-efficient to purchase neem oil in pour bottles, you will also want to get a spray bottle from your local dollar store. This is one of those purchases that many indoor gardeners assume they won't need, but they quickly regret not investing in neem oil when they lose their fruits and veggies to a preventable cause like fungi.

Although you will want to have a thermometer for reading the temperature of your grow space, you will also want a soil thermometer to get a crystal-clear sense of how your plants are doing. You can always get one and use it to test the soil of your various pots from time to time. However, most are cheap enough that it makes more sense just to purchase one for each container, and leave it in place so that you can always check the soil temperature at a glance. Speaking of the soil, it is a good idea to get a test kit so that you can check the pH level of your pots. The pH level basically gives you an understanding of the nutrients and the chemical balance of the soil. Most plants want it to be between 5.5 to 7.5, with the majority right around the middle of that range. Test kits tend to come with several uses but run out quickly. Many gardeners will want to invest in an electronic pH reader to save money and time in the long run.

Once you have these tools, you will have all of the essentials necessary to bring your first plants from seed to harvest. As you grow accustomed to working with your indoor garden, you are likely to discover new tools that will make your life easier, but these can be purchased as the need arises.

INDOOR GARDENING

Chapter Summary

- Starting a new garden means getting your hands on a lot of gear, but each piece has a purpose and will make your life a lot less stressful. It will ensure that your plants produce the largest harvest possible.

- Different plants require different sized containers. You will most likely want to purchase a couple of 10 or 14-inch containers for seeding your vegetables.

- The chances are that if you are looking to grow the more traditional vegetables such as cucumbers, peppers, eggplants, tomatoes, or broccoli, then you will be using either an 18 or 24-inch pot.

- You should only need a 30-inch pot if you are growing large plants like rhubarb or pumpkins. Keep in mind that these larger plants weigh more, and so the material of your 30-inch pot needs to be durable enough to support them.

- Pots come in all sorts of designs that can end up costing a lot, but your plants won't grow any better in an expensive pot than they would in a cheap one. Just make sure that whatever container you use has drainage holes.

- Many growers like wooden pots, but given that they slowly break down and the way that water

INDOOR GARDENING

can damage them, it is better to go with plastic, ceramic, or terracotta.

- Ceramic pots are heavy and expensive but quite durable. Terracotta is cheaper than ceramic and also quite durable, but they tend to dry out quicker than other types.

- Plastic pots are the cheapest and break rather easily, but they are the ones most growers go to for their light weight and affordability.

- If you want the best taking fruits and vegetables, then you really should use an organic potting mix. You can find pre-made ones at any garden store.

- A good potting soil is made up of three parts: a growing medium, a material for retaining moisture, and another to allow draining.

- You can make your homemade potting soil by combining equal parts garden soil (for growing), peat moss (moisture retention), and either sand, perlite, or vermiculite (drainage).

- You can also make an effective potting soil by combining equal parts garden soil and compost. Just make sure the compost is made out of vegetable scraps, bread, eggshells, cardboard, and fruit scraps. Avoid animal products in your garden compost as this attracts disease and hungry critters. Add sand to this mixture so it can drain.

INDOOR GARDENING

- Plants suck nutrients out of the soil, so you will want to add fertilizer over time. You can always purchase fertilizer at the store, or you can top dress your plants with your compost mix.

- While it is necessary to have a fan for airflow and a humidifier to keep your grow space at 40%-50%, these don't need to be top of the line or overly expensive models. You can always use a timer to control when they turn off and on.

- Light comes in warm and cold temperatures. The higher the K number, the colder the light. Your garden will want light in the 3000K range.

- Fluorescent grow lights are fine for one or two plants. HID grow lights are good for several plants but they're also expensive and consume a lot of power. LED lights are the best choice for those that want to save money because they last longer and take up less electricity.

- Provide your plants with 50 watts of light per square foot. Multiply the square footage of your garden by 50 to find the total number of watts you will require.

- You will want to purchase a watering can, garden shears, a small rake, a spade, and a trowel. A spray bottle and some neem oil is an absolute must. You should also get some soil thermometers and either a pH test kit or an electronic pH reader.

INDOOR GARDENING

In the next chapter, you will learn all about the operating cycle of your indoor vegetable or fruit garden. From seeding to watering and fertilizing, you will learn exactly what goes into maintaining your garden and keeping it healthy from seed to harvest.

CHAPTER THREE

THE OPERATION CYCLE OF AN INDOOR GARDEN

Now that you have everything that you need for your garden, it is time to put everything together and get your hands dirty! Since the most common way that gardeners start out is by planting seeds, we will begin with a look at how to raise our fruits and veggies from seed to seedling and then transplant them from the seeding container to the containers you have set out for your garden proper. From there, we will move onto the rest of the operation cycle, such aspects as watering and fertilizing your plants.

With the knowledge in this chapter, you will know what goes into raising your plants. Then the next three chapters will look at fruits, vegetables, and herbs, respectively. These chapters will each focus on the type of plant in question and go into specifics about them there. However, all of the plants looked at in the

INDOOR GARDENING

following chapters are raised properly by following the operation cycle laid out in this chapter.

Soiling Your Pots to Seed Your Garden

In the last chapter, we saw two ways to make our own potting soil. Of course, you can always go to your local gardening center and purchase pre-made potting soil as well, the choice of which to use is entirely yours. Regardless of which you go with, however, you are going to do pretty much the same thing with it. Fill up the containers that are to be a part of your garden so that the soil is a quarter of an inch from the rim of the pot. Since we are beginning with seeds, it is okay to only worry about filling up the smallest pots that will be used for the seedlings at this stage. Just remember that your seedlings will be moved into larger pots when they are large enough, keep an eye on their growth and add potting mix to your larger containers a day or two ahead of time so that you have everything ready for the transplanting when it is time.

Now that your pots have soil, it is time to turn your attention to the seeds that you want to plant. Assuming that you have already purchased the seeds you want from your local garden center, you could just pop them into your containers and call it a day. But it is always a better idea to help your seeds through the germination process through a little extra work. This is especially true if you are planting seeds with a hard shell such as sweet peas or spinach. You can help your plants to germinate by using one of the following three methods.

The first approach is the use of scarification. In order to help the hard shell of the seed break down properly, take the garden shears you have purchased and scrape the shell with them. You don't want to create any deep scratches that expose the inside of the shell because this can ruin the seed, you only want to slightly damage the outside to make it a little weaker. Another way to do this is to take some sandpaper and gently rub the seed to thin out the shell. If you go with the scarification approach, then you will want to plant these seeds as soon as you finish.

Stratification offers another approach that can help with hard-shelled seeds, though it is more often used for plants outside of the fruit, vegetable, or herb varieties. However, some plants such as lettuce or perennial sweet peas benefit greatly from stratification. These seeds tend to have chemicals present, which makes germination difficult or even impossible. In order to get through their hard shell, you need to use a combination of cold and warm temperatures. The best way to achieve this is by letting the seeds first soak for 24 hours in water. At the end of the soaking period, remove the seeds and put them into a sealable plastic bag with some peat moss or vermiculite and then stick them into a refrigerator. It is a good idea to cut tiny holes in the container to allow some airflow as a lack of airflow promotes mold growth. While the length of time and temperatures that seeds require for this process varies depending on the kind of plant, it typically takes two or three months before they are ready to plant.

The third method is the easiest, and that is to soak the seeds. Seeds that benefit from soaking are those with hard coats like asparagus, carrots, corn, peas, pumpkins, or squash, to name but a few. While these seeds may still grow without the soaking process, it could take them days or weeks to germinate this way. To soak your seeds, simply place them in some lukewarm water for between 12 to 24 hours. When you return to your seeds, you may notice that some of them are now floating. These can be thrown away as they are unlikely to germinate properly. Those that are still sitting peacefully at the bottom of the water will be the ones you plant. Remove your seeds and rinse them off with clean water. We do this to remove any chemicals that were released during the soaking process. Plant these seeds as soon as you finish rinsing them.

Now that you either have soft-shelled seeds ready to plant, or hard-shelled seeds that have been correctly prepared, it is time to sow them into their containers. Create a little hole for your seeds that is between a quarter to half an inch deep. You can have more than one hole in a container so long as there is enough space to keep them about an inch apart. Drop a couple of seeds into each of the holes you have made and then cover them up with soil. You don't want the covering soil to be too tightly packed, as this will make it harder for oxygen to get to the seeds and this can cause your plants to suffocate. You also don't want to make the holes too deep. Otherwise the seedlings may be unable to break out through the top. When a seed germinates, the shell breaks down, and the seedling uses this for energy to dig its way out of the soil. If it is too deep, then they won't have enough vitality to break out. You may want to cover the container with some plastic wrap in order to keep the moisture and humidity levels up. Keep these containers in a warm area, as seeds tend to require more heat than older plants do.

Even though it may be somewhat tedious at this stage, it is in your best interests to keep an eye on your plants every day. Most of the time, there won't be anything to

INDOOR GARDENING

see, just a container with some dirt in it. But before too long, you will notice a tiny stem sticking out of the earth. That stem will then start to grow branches and leaves. Once you spot these leaves, it will be time to transfer the plant to a larger container. We do this because the root system of the plant will run out of room to continue growing in these small containers and that will stunt the growth and even possibly kill the plant.

To transfer your plants to the new container, the first step is to decide which plants will be moved. Because you planted several seeds in these early pots, you will want to ensure that you transplant the strongest of the seedlings. Look to see which plant is growing the most - this will be the one that you want to transfer. You will want to transfer about one plant per container used. So if you made three holes in your containers and dropped the seeds in all three, you will move the strongest of the three and leave the other two behind. Put your hand over the bowl and spread your fingers so that your seedling sticks out between two fingers. Slowly rotate the pot so that the soil starts to fall out but the plant rests against your hand. You want to let the roots of the plant fall out into your hand. Half fill the new container with the same potting soil (always use the same; otherwise the sudden switch will shock the plant), place the plant in and add more soil. You will want the root ball to be only an inch or two from the top of the container; this is done so that there is plenty of space for the roots to continue to grow. If you already have a bowl filled with soil, then you just need to dig out a big enough hole to place the plant in. Add more soil on top of the plant so as to keep it at roughly the same depth that it had been in the first container.

If everything has gone well, then you won't see any issues and your plants will continue their growth unimpeded. Continue checking on them every day and provide the seedlings with the temperature, pH level, humidity, and water that the species needs to grow. When you do this, you will have full-grown plants in no time.

Watering Your Plants

While it is one of the most vital parts of tending for any garden, watering your indoor garden is actually a very easy process. But, since you are growing fruit and vegetables, it is worthwhile to keep in mind that watering is even more important than if you were growing flowers. This is because when they are left to go dry, vegetable plants will produce a weak harvest and may even actually ruin the entire harvest. So, if there is one part of the operation cycle that you absolutely cannot ignore, it is ensuring that your plants are correctly watered. But this isn't an excuse to drown your plants by overwatering them either; you need to be mindful of *when* you water them.

INDOOR GARDENING

Your plants are going to need to be watered frequently, far more often than the same type of plant would require if it was grown in the outdoor earth. This is because potting soil has a tendency to dry out a lot quicker than the soil in your backyard. You will also need to be mindful of the temperature; on days in which the temperature rises, you will need to water more (sometimes even multiple times in a single day). If you are unsure whether or not it is time to water your plants, there are two ways that you can see if they are ready. The first is to simply put your finger into the soil. You should stick your finger deep enough that you submerge the middle phalanx joint in the earth; this is the main joint in your finger after the knuckle. If the soil is dry, then you will want to water. The other way to check is to lift the container or tip it slightly onto its side. Try doing this when you first water the plants and then later to monitor them. You will notice that the container is much lighter when it is dry, so this simple weight check lets you know if it is time to water.

It is necessary to ensure that you thoroughly water your plants. When potting soil is dry, it can actually be a bit of a pain to effectively water it. The root ball will sometimes move away from the sides of the container when it is dry, and this creates a situation that when you water the plant, all of the water goes down the sides of the container in the divots that the roots leave behind. You can get around this issue by always watering your plants so that the water level rises to the top of the container. Doing this guarantees the roots of your plant get plenty of water. However, this can easily lead to drowning the plant, so it is worth checking the soil first to make sure it is the right time to water.

Keep in mind that there is a difference between dry soil and moist soil. When you remove your finger from the potting mix, moist soil will stick to it. If this happens, then it isn't yet time to water. While vegetable plants should never be left to dry out, it's an excellent idea to always read the instructions that come with the seeds, as well as asking an employee at your local gardening center. Browse reliable Internet sites for the best care practices for that species. Different plants have different water needs, so always inform yourself about the needs of your plant first rather than just assume what is best for them.

INDOOR GARDENING

Fertilizing Your Indoor Garden

Human beings need to drink and eat. When we consider watering, it is clear that plants also need to drink lots of fluids. But as it so happens, plants also need to eat. Only they need their nutrients to come from the soil or a liquid fertilizer. The roots of your plants stretch out underneath the soil, spreading in order to seek out more food to provide all the nutrients that they need to keep growing nice and healthy. If you are raising your plants in the ground outdoors, then those roots can stretch a good distance and find lots of nutrients. But when you raise those same plants indoors, there is only so much space in each container that they can spread out, and there are only so many nutrients in the soil. To make certain your indoor plants eat their fill, you need to fertilize them on a regular basis.

Regardless of what potting soil you decide to use, your plants will suck it dry of nutrients in less than two months. When this happens, they will begin to starve. You can buy time in this process by adding a slow-release fertilizer or manure pellets (such as chicken) into the soil. However, these are only going to buy your plants a certain amount of breathing space. They won't be enough on their own to keep your plants from starving. For that, you are going to need to create a schedule to regularly feed your plants a liquid fertilizer. There are many liquid fertilizers available on the market that you can purchase, or you can make your own. We'll see how to make our own in a moment, but before we do, it is a good idea to understand what exactly a fertilizer is providing for your plants. By gaining a knowledge of this, you have the best possible understanding of what they require.

The majority of fertilizers available are primarily focused on providing three nutrients to your plants: nitrogen, phosphorus, and potassium, or NPK. I say the majority of fertilizers because there are a decent amount on the market those focuses on only one of these three nutrients rather than all three. You can also purchase these nutrients on their own in a solid form meant to be dissolved in water. However, if you are purchasing pre-made fertilizer for your indoor garden, then the best idea is to choose a fertilizer that has an NPK ratio with equal amounts of each nutrient. Of course, it is rare that it is always a one for one ratio, and so it is okay for the ratio to be a little uneven so long as the nutrients are present in approximately equal quantities. If you are growing fruit or plants that fruit such as strawberries, raspberries, tomatoes, or peppers, then you are going to want to use a fertilizer with a higher amount of potassium as this helps the plants to grow their fruits properly. When using a store-bought fertilizer, you should always follow the instructions on the package so that you avoid overfeeding. When you overfeed them, the pH level in the soil rises to high levels. If you bought soil testing kits or an electronic pH reader, then you should keep a close eye on the pH level.

Buying fertilizer can quickly become expensive if you have a large garden to maintain. One way around this rising cost is to make your own. But be aware that it is always a very smelly process! One way to quickly get yourself some fertilizer is to fill a bag up with compost and let it soak in water for ten days. On day ten, you add water to the mixture until the color changes from black to slightly gray like tea, at which point it is ready to use. Another simple fertilizer uses urine as the primary ingredient since it is sterile, has a decent amount of potassium, and a lot of nitrogen in it, plus it's very easy to acquire because you can use your own! Dilute one part urine with forty parts water, and you have yourself a quick and efficient fertilizer. However, although this method is a little more difficult, you may be interested in making a comfrey fertilizer due to its high potassium concentration. The same steps you take to make a comfrey fertilizer can be used to make a nettle or a borage fertilizer if you need a higher nitrogen count.

Comfrey is a herb from Europe that has high levels of potassium, phosphorus, and nitrogen. That means this one herb can provide you with all the NPK you need from a fertilizer. There are ways to turn this into a fine fertilizer, but it's necessary to note that what is really great about comfrey is that you can grow it yourself as a part of your herb garden so that you can always have plenty of source material to turn into fertilizer. It is pretty much one of the best investments you can make when it comes to feeding your plants. When there is too much carbon in a plant bed, this can make it hard for the plants to get the best benefits from the nitrogen in the soil. Comfrey has a carbon-nitrogen ratio that is perfect in preventing any of these issues.

To make fertilizer out of comfrey, all you need to do is stuff a bunch of comfrey leaves into a large container. Cut a little hole in the bottom of the container, and put a smaller bowl underneath to catch the black liquid that drips out. It takes a few weeks to start producing this black liquid, though it can be sped up by using a heavy object to press down on the leaves. This liquid is excellent for fertilizer when you mix it with water in a 15:1 ratio. That's all it takes to make comfrey fertilizer, but there is more you can do with comfrey around your garden. Take the leaves out after the pressing and use them to feed your potatoes or tomatoes as a nutritious mulch. As long as you let comfrey leaves wilt for a few days first, it can be used in this manner. You can also add comfrey leaves to the containers you are planning to use next to add more nutrients to the initial soil. Make sure you are using it with slightly older plants and not young seedlings as it can be too strong for them and lead to nutrient burn. Finally, you can add comfrey leaves to your compost to help make it more nutritious.

If you purchased your fertilizer, then it will have instructions on how often to use it, and you should always listen to these instructions. However, if you have created your own, then you are going to need to educate yourself on the needs of the particular plants you are looking to feed. Some, such as fruiting veggies like tomatoes or peppers, will benefit from a weekly feeding schedule. However, there are others, such as lettuce, which don't need a regular fertilizer feed. You should always research your plants before seeding them by either Googling the information or asking your local garden center employees. Also, you shouldn't try to give fertilizer to plants that are overly stressed out. While it may seem like a good idea to dose them with fertilizer to help them get better, it is actually much less stressful on the plant to be given clean water instead. You also won't need to use liquid fertilizer on your herbs, as they generally grow best by being light on nutrients.

INDOOR GARDENING

INDOOR GARDENING

Chapter Summary

- Start your seeds first in a smaller receptacle, filling the bowl up with soil so that it is a quarter of an inch from the top.

- Soft-shelled seeds can simply be placed into a hole and covered with earth, but hard- shelled seeds need to either go through scarification, stratification or soaking to weaken their shells enough for germination to happen.

- Scarification is done by gently scraping the outer layer of the seeds or by using a coarse sandpaper to file them down. It is important not to go so hard as to expose the inside of the seed. If this happens then the seed is ruined.

- Stratification is a two-step process of first soaking seeds for 24 hours and then storing them in a refrigerator. Put seeds in a sealable bag filled with peat moss or vermiculite and stick them in the fridge for two or three months until they begin to germinate, at which point you plant them in a container.

- Soaking is the easiest method as all you need to do is leave your seeds in water for 12 to 24 hours. Remove any seeds that have floated to the top, as these are no longer viable, and plants those that have remained on the bottom.

- When planting seeds, drop a couple into each hole you make for them. Even those that have

INDOOR GARDENING

passed the soaking test may not germinate properly. Plant multiple seeds and then transplant those that seem to have most vitality into bigger pots once they are large enough.

- Fruits and vegetables need plenty of water to grow properly, but too much will drown the plants. The best way to tell if a plant is ready to be watered is by performing the finger test: simply stick your finger an inch or two into the soil to see if the top inch (sometimes top two inches depending on the needs of the plant) is dry. A dry top inch means it is time to water.

- Roots will often spread out to the sides of a bowl but then shrink back into the middle when the plant is too dry. This leaves holes along the side of the containers that water can run through, which leaves your plants thirsty despite having just been watered. Because of this, always make sure that you thoroughly water the plants each and every time you do.

- To tell the difference between dry soil and moist soil, use the finger test, and see if any soil sticks to your finger when it is removed. If the soil sticks, then it is moist, not dry.

- Plants need to drink plenty of water to grow but they also need to eat plenty of nutrients. Specifically, they really need nitrogen, phosphorus, and potassium (NPK). The best fertilizers are liquid fertilizers that use natural ingredients to create an even balance between these three nutrients.

- Adding manure pellets or compost to your soil is one way to naturally increase the amount of nutrients present. Just remember to keep a close eye on the pH level of your soil, as too much will lead to nutrient burn and damage your plants.

- Store-bought fertilizers can cost a lot of money, but it is easy to make your own. One approach is to leave a bag of compost to soak in water for ten days and then add more water until the mix is a light gray color. Another approach is to mix one part urine with forty parts water.

- The absolute best fertilizer that you can make yourself comes from seeping the liquid from comfrey herb and mixing this liquid in a ratio of one part comfrey juice to 15 parts water. Comfrey leaves also work well when they're mixed into compost or fed to your plants in the form of mulch.

- Some plants like to be fertilized on a weekly basis, such as tomatoes or peppers, while others require far less, such as lettuce.

In the next chapter, you will learn what it takes to grow fruit inside your home. We'll look at why organic fruit is so highly regarded, and we'll go over how to produce your own strawberries, oranges, peaches and more.

INDOOR GARDENING

You'll love how you can have your favorite fruits without the hassle of going to the store.

CHAPTER FOUR

GROWING BEAUTIFUL FRUITS

Everything you need to know about maintaining your garden has been covered already, so now it is time to finally get into the plants themselves. Up first are the fruits, the tastiest plants of all. You'll learn what it takes to grow healthy fruit plants with large yields. There isn't enough room in this book to cover every type of fruit, so we'll stick to some of the most popular to see exactly what goes into raising delicious strawberries, peaches and more.

Just a note: While tomatoes are technically a fruit, we'll be looking at them in the next chapter. You add tomatoes to a garden salad, not a fruit punch, after all!

Why Organic Foods are Better

Going organic has become a fashionable trend these days, with more and more people jumping aboard the organic train. But going organic is more than just a trend that will pass with time. There are numerous benefits to growing and eating such foods rather than pumping your garden (and your dinner table) full of every kind of chemical imaginable. The benefits of organic fruit and produce are most recognizable at the wider level of farming and industry movements. However, there are many benefits lower down the chain that beneficially affects the people that eat these foods. Let's take a look at these now.

The main thing that separates organic foods from the rest is the lack of chemicals. There are no harmful GMOs used when growing organic. This is great since many GMOs are used alongside other harmful chemicals in modern farming practices these days. Purchasing organic foods supports farmers that care about the long-term consequences of the food they produce, and removes money from the hands of organizations willing to jeopardize your health for profit. It also reinforces healthier soil, slows the growth of super strains, saves taxpayer money (in the form of subsidies for non-organic farmers), and it keeps harmful chemicals from seeping into the oceans. But what benefits does organic farming provide you as an indoor gardener? Strictly speaking, there are four answers to that question.

The first benefit is the taste. A stressed plant tastes bad - it is just a fact. A lot of the GMO produced crops are under a lot of stress, and you can tell the difference when you compare a GMO grown fruit to one that has been organically grown. Stressed-out plants need to spend their energy repairing themselves and searching out more nutrients. Meanwhile, a healthy organically grown plant can concentrate its strength on producing the best fruit possible. That, in turn, means juicier, larger, tastier fruits (and veggies!), and this is wonderful news for your taste buds.

Organic foods also have more nutrients and antioxidants than those grown through chemical processes. Therefore, the fruits you are growing organically in your apartment are going to be super-great for you and your health. The extra nutrients come from the soil that is employed in organic growing. We aim to use compost and natural fertilizers to keep our potting soil nutrient-rich for our fruits and vegetables, and this shows its benefits in the nutrient content of the fruits we produce. Fruit developed organically typically has 30% more antioxidants when compared to GMO grown products. That's a huge increase when you remember that organic fruit also tastes better. Not only does it taste better but it *is* better for you, period.

Growing organic food promotes a healthier lifestyle in general. It is my belief that, when you see how great the food from your indoor garden tastes, you'll agree. Many gardeners enjoy sharing their harvest with friends and family and this, in turn, spreads the joys of organic farming to more people. Once people have experienced how much more delicious your fruits are, they are that much more likely to reach for the organically grown produce next time they are shopping. That means more money flowing into healthy farming practices that promote wellness. Plus, when you are growing your own fruit, you can't help but become that much more involved in what you put in your body, and this leads to people making healthier choices regarding their wellbeing and fitness.

Finally, growing organic fruits and vegetables will teach you about how much further products can go. Most people toss out their compost and never spend even a second thinking about how it could be used. Once you start saving your compost for your crops and studying the ways you can make use of your plants (such as the many benefits of comfrey), you will realize there are many more uses for the goods around you than you ever previously imagined. These factors promote a lifestyle that is more sustainable and gets as much use out of the stuff around you as is possible. While this may seem an odd reason to favor organic fruit, this subtle shift in perspective is bound to have a major impact on your carbon footprint and the way you consider waste.

Growing Gorgeous Strawberries

Strawberries are a favorite of indoor gardeners and not just because of their delicious taste. Rather, they are a favorite because they are easy to grow almost anywhere, whether that is sitting on your windowsill, or set into a vertical growing setup along a wall. They aren't particularly large plants, which makes them quite versatile. While they are best grown at a temperature between 68F or 77F, they can grow at both warmer or colder temperatures as well. You should note, while they can tolerate temperatures outside of the normal, what they can't tolerate are sudden changes in the temperature. When strawberry plants are forced to experience drastic temperature drops, they can get stressed to the point of damage, and they will produce a dramatically reduced yield when it comes time to harvest. Strawberries are able to grow in the shade but they much prefer to have direct light.

The unique thing about growing strawberries indoors is that you actually have to pollinate them yourselves. When growing outdoors, the best way to pollinate strawberry plants is by using honey bees. However, this is clearly not an option indoors! But the pollination still has to happen or you won't get any berries. So, in order to ensure a good harvest, you need to pollinate your strawberries by hand. You will know that your plants are ready to be pollinated when the petals of the strawberry flowers open up completely. Strawberry plants have gendered parts with a greenish-yellow female part (the pistil) and a brown male part (the stamen). The procedure to follow is as follows: take a small brush, like those used for makeup, and brush the pollen from the stamen down into the pistil. Do this for each and every flower on the plant. You want to make sure that the entire pistil is covered, otherwise you will end up with misshapen and deformed berries that are rather unappealing. Many gardeners go over each flower twice so that they can be super-sure that everything has been correctly pollinated. You can pollinate the flowers every day if you want (and many people do). When the white petals of the flower start to die off and leave green leaves (called sepal), then you know the pollination was successful, and you will soon have strawberries growing.

When it comes to watering strawberry plants, how much they require depends on what part of the growth cycle they've reached. In the early stages, they need far less water and typically can go a few days without watering. However, they will need to be watered on a daily basis during the fruiting phase of their life cycle, otherwise they get too dry and produce a poor yield. While watering the plants, keep in mind the pH level of the soil. Strawberries like to have a pH level in the 6.0 to 6.5 range, but they can tolerate a 0.5 difference either way. They use nitrogen to produce healthy leaves, and phosphorous and potassium are used to flower and produce berries. Be careful about the amount of nitrogen your strawberries are receiving; too much will cause the leaves to grow large, but this comes at the cost of fewer flowers, and the berries themselves will be much more susceptible to disease.

Strawberries are prone to the same pests and diseases that most plants have to deal with, and they also attract animals like rats or mice. Birds also love to eat strawberries, but this shouldn't be a problem so long as your windows are closed! Pets are also prone to either eat the berries or dig in the soil. Be mindful of these threats and keep an eye out for giveaway signs such as paw marks in the soil or partially eaten berries or leaves. As long as the berries are kept safe from pests and critters, they can be plucked off the plant and eaten immediately. You will know they are ripe and ready when they reach a beautiful and bold red color.

Growing an Indoor Peach Tree

It may come as a surprise to learn that peach trees actually thrive when grown indoors. While the species grown for peach farming is far too large to fit into most houses, there is such a thing as dwarf peach trees which don't take up nearly as much space. Despite being a smaller variety, these dwarf peach trees have a large enough yield to make it well worth the effort it takes to grow. A dwarf tree, so long as it is properly pruned, can be kept around five feet. Besides pruning, you'll find they are surprisingly easy to take care of.

When picking out a peach tree species to grow, you don't have to worry too much about their preferred climate since you will be raising it indoors. If it is growing in the

INDOOR GARDENING

same location as the rest of your fruits and vegetables, then climate is a concern; otherwise, you can use equipment to provide a perfect growing space for your tree. What is most important is the size of the species of peach tree and whether or not it self-pollinates. Some dwarf species which make for great plants are the golden glory, honey babe, or peregrine trees. Bonsai peach trees also come in manageable sizes, and the autumn red species is particularly delicious.

Once you know what kind of peach tree you want to grow, you then need to decide if you'd like to grow it from a pit or if you want to purchase a young tree. A young tree may be ready for harvest in a year or so, but growing from a pit will take a minimum of three years before your tree starts to grow peaches. If you do decide to grow from a pit, then you will first want to test your pit to ensure it can actually grow. To do this, you just need to drop the pit into a bowl of water and see if it sinks. Just like when hard-shelled seeds float up to the top during soaking, if your peach pit floats, then it is no good. Once your pit passes the sinking test, you should use the stratification method to prepare the seed. Remember, it is always a good idea to prepare more than one pit at a time because even pits that pass the sinking test may not germinate in the right way once they have been planted. You will know that the pits are ready to be planted when they begin to grow roots.

INDOOR GARDENING

While the seedling may seem a little small, you'll want to transplant it to a five gallon pot. Most of the time that we are growing plants, we aim to provide them with a pot that gives them plenty of room to grow. Since this is a tree we are growing indoors, we can help keep the tree a manageable size by using a smaller container like this. Line the bottom of the pot with gravel to promote drainage and to give the container some more weight so that it stays in place. A light container may fall over and collapse under the weight of the tree and, not only is this bad for the health of your tree, it can also cause a major mess in your house. Fill up the rest of the container with your chosen potting mix and make sure to include some compost (especially if it has some comfrey mixed in) to impart plenty of nutrients to the soil. Dig out a little hole to drop your seeds into and gently cover them with the earth. If you waited until the roots started to grow during the stratification process, then you will see your peach tree sticking out of the soil in a few short days.

Peach trees really enjoy their light, and the more you can give them the better they will respond. You should aim to give them six or more hours of light a day. While they will continue to stay healthy with as little as four hours a day, you will notice a much smaller yield, and it will take far longer for them to grow. Most peach trees will want a temperature of 75F during the summer, and a temperature of 45F during the winter. Peach trees go dormant during the winter, and they require this reduction in temperature to maintain their health. If you keep the temperature high during their dormant period, then you are only going to damage the tree. You can't just trick your peach tree into skipping winter; you need to learn to work with the schedule that it sets for you.

How often your peach tree needs to be watered will also depend on the season. Plants grown inside need to be watered more often than those grown in the earth, and peach trees are no different in this regard. During the summer period, you can expect to water your tree every day or two. During the winter, the need for water is far less, and you can find yourself going a week or two between watering. Use the finger test to check how dry the soil is to determine whether or not it is time to water.

INDOOR GARDENING

You will want to check the top two inches of the earth when it comes to peach trees, so put your finger in up to the knuckle. Indoor peach trees also require more fertilizer than those grown outdoors. Fertilizing should happen every other week. Use a fertilizer that is high in phosphorus. A good rule of thumb to remember is that if the fertilizer is good for tomato plants, then it is good for your peach tree. You don't need to fertilize your tree during the dormant period, only during the growing season.

You will want to prune your tree on a yearly basis. Doing this helps to keep the tree from growing too big, and it will also eventually lead to new branches that will go on to produce more delicious peaches. Wait until the buds of your tree begin to show some pink blooms and then trim. You'll find this occurs near the start of the growing period. You do not want to prune your peach tree during its dormant phase, as this is an extra stressful time for it to undergo that kind of shock. Peaches grow on young branches, those around one year in age, so you can expect to prune a good 40% of the branches away every year. Dead branches, damaged branches, or diseased branches should all be removed at this time. If you notice branches that are starting to shoot off and grow upwards, then you may want to remove these as well. When you remove those branches that are growing upwards the plant begins to focus its energy on expanding outwards instead, and so this is a good way to prevent the tree from getting too tall. If you are growing a self-pollinating tree, then you don't need to worry about the flowers at this stage. If you need to manually pollinate your tree, then you can follow the steps listed above on how to deal with strawberry plants.

You will notice a lot of little peaches beginning to grow on your plant. While this will look like a wonderful yield, you are going to want to remove some of these peaches. Wait until they are about an inch in size, and then remove any peaches that have clustered together so that there are about 4 or 5 inches between each peach. This may seem like a weird thing to do, reducing the size of your yield, but what you are doing is making it easier for the remaining peaches to get enough energy to grow big and healthy. You will find this produces bigger, juicier peaches. The peaches are ready to be harvested when they start to smell like a peach should. Give a peach a squeeze: if it is still hard, then it isn't ready, but if it squishes then it is.

INDOOR GARDENING

Caring for Indoor Oranges

Most people don't consider the possibility of growing an orange tree indoors. Yet fruits of the citrus variety take quickly to indoor growing conditions. So long as you are able to provide your orange tree with the right environment, you will be able to produce delicious oranges inside your own home. It is especially rewarding to grow oranges indoors because of the wonderful fragrances that these plants produce. It is like having a natural air freshener in your living room.

As with peaches, you will want to choose one of the varieties of orange tree that is considered to be a dwarf offshoot of those trees that are grown outdoors. You need to live in a very specific climate to grow oranges outdoors, but thanks to modern technology, we are able to create whatever conditions our trees need when raised indoors. Some species of orange tree that grow quite well indoors are Tahitian, satsuma, or calamondin oranges. The Tahitian produces very sweet oranges that are quite small, almost a mixture of a tangerine and a lemon. The satsuma tree produces tangerines and has quite a strange fragrance. The calamondin orange tree produces a small fruit that has a tangy, sour taste. Of the three, the calamondin is the type most often grown indoors.

Orange seeds are of the hard-shell variety, but they are much easier to plant when compared to the peach tree seed. While the peach tree seed takes several months of preparation due to their need for stratification, orange tree seeds only need to undergo the soaking process. If you set your seeds to soak before you go to bed, they will be ready for planting by lunchtime the following day. Just remember to toss out any seeds that are floating on top of the water. Plant your seeds in your starting pot, ensuring that the soil mixture has plenty of vermiculite, perlite, sand, or gravel to promote drainage.

You will need to transfer the young tree into a bigger container when you start to see leaves sticking out of the soil. Some gardeners suggest repotting orange trees once every couple of years. If you notice that the soil is drying out faster than normal, start seeing the roots of the tree sticking out of the drainage holes of its container, or the leaves begin to look unhealthy, then these are all signs that it is time to transplant your tree to a different container. Pick out a larger container and wait for spring, as this is the best time to transfer the tree. Much like the peach tree, it is harmful to transplant orange trees during the offseason. To properly repot your tree, you should first wait until the soil has dried out, which should take only a day or two. Using your garden tools, carefully break the earth away from the edges of the container so that nothing is sticking to the pot. Grasp the trunk of the tree as close to the soil as you can and very carefully lift the tree out of the bowl, and place it into the new container, which should be roughly a quarter filled with soil. Add more soil over the top of the roots of the tree and then immediately water the tree. Because you had to allow the tree to dry out before moving it, it is important that you make sure it has plenty of water over the next couple of weeks and doesn't go dry again. The period after replanting your orange tree is very stressful to it, and you want to pay extra close attention to its needs during this time.

INDOOR GARDENING

Orange trees have a complicated relationship with water. When it comes to the container they are housed in, orange trees want good drainage and plenty of aeration for the roots. They also want a bowl that can hold plenty of moisture, so containers made out of terracotta, wood, or ceramics will definitely require extra attention to ensure the trees don't dry out. The best way to figure out how regularly to water your tree is to pay attention to how rapidly the soil dries out. Each tree has a mind of its own when it comes to how quickly it uses up its water. A good habit when starting out is to perform the finger test twice a day, once in the morning and once at night. This will give you a clear picture of how quickly your tree uses water, and once you have that, you can create a schedule accordingly. When watering, always ensure the water soaks into the soil, and doesn't just dribble down the sides of the container. Keep in mind that, just like peach trees, your orange tree has different watering needs depending on the season. Orange trees require more water in spring and summer, though overwatering them is a recipe for root rot. Even when they are the thirstiest, avoid excessively watering them. They will require much less water in the fall and winter, and it is best to wait until the finger test reveals a dry top inch rather than a mostly dry one. When it comes to checking the dryness of your trees, it is all about the top inch of the soil. The roots should never be allowed to dry out, though you will probably only need to water an orange tree a few times a week when warm, and once every week

INDOOR GARDENING

or so when cold. Finally, be careful to make sure the temperature of the water is matched to the temperature of the plant. Watering an orange tree with hotter or colder water stresses out an orange tree, and that results in a poorer yield and lower quality fruit.

Since orange trees are primarily grown in tropical weather, they will want to have a higher humidity level than many of the other plants in your indoor garden. Where most garden plants prefer a humidity level between 40% and 50%, your orange tree is going to want the humidity to be between 50% and 70%. Achieving this indoors isn't always simple, and too much heat during the colder months will damage the tree. One way that you can help your orange tree to achieve this is by misting the leaves on a regular basis; this practice, when combined with the use of a humidifier, should be enough to keep your tree healthy. As far as heat is concerned, an orange tree considers 68F to be the perfect temperature. Sudden changes in the temperature will harm it, so it is best to keep it away from windows where sunlight will overheat it, or a windy draft will cool it off. That said, orange trees like a slight drop in temperature during the night, usually down somewhere between 63F or 58F.

Orange trees like to be in very bright areas, but they don't enjoy getting direct sunlight. Instead, they grow best when they receive about eight hours of indirect light a day. Just like human beings burn when we stay out in the sun too long, direct sunlight can cause burns to the leaves of an orange tree. If you are providing lighting for your trees through electronic means, then you don't need to worry as much about direct or indirect light, just so long as the grow lamps you have purchased don't run too hot. LEDs are particularly perfect for orange trees; they provide plenty of wattage without a massive amount of excess heat.

Your tree will require lots of nutrients in order to grow and fruit to its best potential. A pH level between 6.0 and 7.5 is ideal. You can expect to use a liquid fertilizer on your tree once every week during the growing season. Unlike peach trees, orange trees continue to grow all year long rather than go dormant, but they do reduce the speed of their growth during the fall and winter. The fact that they don't become inactive means that you will need to continue fertilizing them all year round. However, you should change the feeding schedule to every other week instead. Oranges are a citrus fruit like lemons or grapefruit, and these species need more micronutrients than many of the other plants in your indoor garden. It is best to purchase a citrus fertilizer that has plenty of zinc, iron, manganese, and magnesium in it. Of course, you don't want to sacrifice the NPK content of your fertilizer, either. Given that citrus requires such a specific diet, it is better to seek out a specially designed fertilizer rather than create your own.

An orange tree doesn't need to be pruned as often as a peach tree does. If you are going to prune your tree, you should wait until branches are at least four inches before removing them. You should also prune in the warmer months to control the direction of growth. In the colder months, pruning should be done to remove damaged or sick branches so as to promote a healthier tree. You will notice that during the colder months, especially at the start of the new year, your orange tree begins to lose leaves. This time of year is often hard on the tree, and it is very important to pay close attention to how many leaves it is losing. A few leaves aren't a big deal, but anything above a few is a sign that there are environmental issues that need to be addressed. If you notice that the leaves are turning yellow, then this is not an environmental issue, but rather a telltale sign that there is a nutrient deficiency that needs to be dealt with.

Finally, your orange tree will begin to flower in the colder months of the year. You will be able to tell this is happening not only by the gorgeous white blossoms that start to open up on the tree but also by the strong fragrance of citrus that they produce. When the flowers begin to bloom, it is time to get out your trusty pollinating brush and get to work. Go over each blossom twice to ensure that everything is pollinated effectively (the same as you do with strawberries). As long as you look after the environmental, watering, and nutritional needs of your orange tree and do your best to avoid causing it unnecessary stress, then you will have delicious homegrown oranges in no time.

Chapter Summary

- More than being merely a fashionable trend, organic farming techniques remove harmful GMOs from our food. They also reduce the amount of poisonous chemicals seeping into our oceans, remove money from the hands of chemical farmers and puts it into the hands of those that care about natural growing, reduces the growth of super strains, saves taxpayer money and promotes healthier soil.

- For the indoor gardener, the benefits of organically grown foods are just as significant. Organically grown fruits and vegetables don't undergo as much stress as chemically grown ones do, and this allows for much tastier harvests. The number of nutrients and antioxidants in organically grown food is also much higher than those that are chemically developed. Taking the time to grow organically promotes both a healthier lifestyle and a more sustainable one too.

- Strawberries require a temperature between 68F and 77F. Just make sure that whatever temperature you pick stays consistent, or your plants can be damaged through the stress of changing.

- Strawberries need to be pollinated by hand. Take a makeup or paintbrush and brush the pollen from the stamen of the strawberry blossom into the pistil. Do this for every blossom on the plant and then go over them a second time to ensure an even spread.

- Strawberries can go a few days without water in the early stages of growth but will require daily watering when they begin to fruit. They want a soil pH at the 6.0 to 6.5 level and need extra nitrogen while vegetative, but extra potassium and phosphorus when flowering and fruiting. When fruiting, reduce their nitrogen intake, or you will end up with a smaller harvest that is more prone to disease.

- To grow a peach tree indoors, it is a good idea to choose a dwarf variety, such as the golden glory, honey babe, or peregrine. Bonsai trees, such as the autumn red, also stay within a nice size range for indoor gardeners.

- To grow from a seed, you are going to need to stratificate the seeds prior to planting. Peach seeds will take a couple of months in refrigeration before they are ready to be planted. It is a good idea to prepare several seeds at one time in case one of them doesn't properly germinate.

- Use either a heavyweight container or line the bottom of your container with gravel. Gravel will promote better drainage while also weighing the container down so the weight of the tree doesn't collapse it on you. Fill the rest of the container with potting mix and compost.

INDOOR GARDENING

- Peach trees want at least six hours of light a day, a temperature of 75F in the summer, and 45F during their dormant winter phase. Keeping the temperature high during the winter phase will damage the tree.

- Peach trees need to be watered every day or two during the summer and once every week or two during the winter. The finger test will let you know when it is time to water, just make sure to check the top two inches for peach trees.

- Fertilize your peach tree every other week during the summer. You don't need to fertilize them at all during the winter. Pruning your tree to control the direction of growth should happen at the start of the growing season while pruning to remove dead branches should take place during winter. Avoid pruning for growth during the dormant phase, as this only hurts the tree. Peaches only like to grow on new branches, so you can expect to remove 40% of the branches every year to promote the growth of new ones and create a bigger harvest.

- Cut off peaches that are clustered close together so that there are 4 to 5 inches between each peach. That allows the tree to spend its energy better and helps ensure each peach is as tasty as possible.

- Orange trees also grow very well indoors, though you will want to select a dwarf breed such as Tahitian, satsuma, or calamondin oranges. Calamondin is the variety most often chosen for indoor growing.

- Orange seeds need to be soaked overnight before planting. Any that float to the top of the water should be thrown out. After 12 hours, you should plant the seeds directly into a mixture with plenty of vermiculite, perlite, sand, or gravel to allow for good drainage.

- Young orange trees should be transferred to a larger container when you see leaves stick out of the soil. Ensure that the bowl or box you pick has plenty of drainage holes. To repot an orange tree, stop watering it for two days ahead of time so that the soil dries out. Carefully transfer the tree to the new container and water it immediately. Make certain you don't let a freshly transplanted orange tree go thirsty for the weeks immediately following the transplantation as this is a very vulnerable time for the tree.

- Orange trees like containers and soil that hold a lot of moisture, but they also prefer that moisture to drain rather quickly. They require more water in the summer and less in the winter, just be careful not to dehydrate them or to waterlog them. Perform the finger test often so that you never allow the roots of the tree to dry out. You can expect to water a few times a week in summer and once a week in the cold. Make sure the water is the same temperature as the tree's environment.

INDOOR GARDENING

- Keep the temperature of your orange tree around 68F during the day and 63F or 58F at night. Maintain humidity between 50% and 70%. Misting the leaves of the tree with fresh water can help achieve this. Be careful of sudden changes in the temperature, as this greatly stresses out orange trees.

- Orange trees want a pH level between 6.0 and 7.5, and they like to be fertilized on a weekly basis while growing. Orange trees don't go dormant, but they do slow their growth in the colder seasons, so you can expect to have to fertilize them all year round. It is best to use a fertilizer designed for citrus as orange trees require extra zinc, iron, manganese, and magnesium.

- You shouldn't prune an orange tree often. If you are planning to prune to control the direction of growth, then allow branches to reach four inches first and prune in the warmer months of the year. Pruning should only happen in the colder months to remove sick branches.

- During the colder months, you may notice leaves dropping off your orange tree. A few leaves aren't anything to worry about, but when a lot start to come off, this would suggest an environmental issue. If the leaves are turning yellow, then there is a nutrient deficiency to be addressed.

INDOOR GARDENING

- Orange trees flower during the colder months. Pollinate the flowers in the same way as you did the strawberries. You will have delicious oranges to eat in no time at all.

In the next chapter, you will learn what it takes to cultivate the most delicious organic vegetables imaginable. From tomatoes to cucumbers, eggplants to lettuce, you can grow all the vegetables necessary to get your three daily servings (and then some!).

CHAPTER FIVE

CULTIVATING DELICIOUS VEGETABLES

Although fruits, thanks to their natural sugars, are the sweetest of the plants you can grow indoors, most gardeners in our position, are primarily interested in growing vegetables, Why? Well, they're versatile, and they provide tons of nutritional value. We already saw that organically grown fruits produce more nutritious harvests; when you combine this increase in yield with the health benefits that come from eating plenty of vegetables, it's easy to see why growing your vegetables is a great choice. But not only is it healthy, it is also super fun!

The best part of growing vegetables indoors is that there is no offseason. You can have delicious tomatoes and cucumbers, even during the harshest of winters. Vegetables aren't going to grow in the ground when there is ten feet of snow covering it, but they will certainly grow in your home setup. Many of the vegetables you purchase from the grocery store during the winter are expensive, even though they may be lower quality products. With your indoor garden, you never have to be overcharged for less than perfect veggies again. So let's turn our attention to what it takes to raise indoor tomatoes (the fruit that, quite honestly, should have been born a vegetable!).

Tending Tasty Tomatoes

The first step to growing indoor tomatoes is to pick the variety you are going to raise. Just as we choose a dwarf species for a peach or orange tree, it is best to choose a smaller type of tomato such as a cherry or a plum tomato. While these tomatoes are smaller in size, the plants yield a large number of them. Their smaller size also means they have less skin overall, and so they can grow at a quicker speed than larger species. Some species of tomatoes that make a great addition to an indoor garden are pink ping pong, Siberia, micro tom, totem, red robin, or patio tomatoes. Most species of tomato take about 70 days to grow, though this can vary by 20 days on either end, depending what you choose. There are a lot of growers that try using chemical fertilizers to make their tomatoes grow faster so that they can make a quick profit off them. This non-organic approach results in tomatoes with a very bland taste, exactly the kind of thing we aim to avoid by growing organically.

INDOOR GARDENING

Go ahead and add your potting mixture to the containers you are going to be starting your seeds in. While it isn't essential for the seed containers, you may want to include some hydrated lime in the primary growing receptacle (at a ratio of roughly one teaspoon per gallon of soil). This addition will change the pH level in the soil, so be mindful of that while mixing, but the calcium it adds to the potting mix will help to prevent blossom end rot, which could significantly damage your plants down the road. Tomato seeds don't need to be prepared prior to planting. To plant them, simply dig a little hole about a quarter of an inch down into the soil, and drop a couple of seeds in. Keep these holes at least an inch from each other if you are planning to raise multiple seedlings in the same container. You can use plastic wrap or a cover for the container to help keep the seed containers from drying out. A temperature of 80F is ideal for germination, and you can expect to notice seedlings poking out of the soil anywhere between one to two weeks from planting. You should remove the plastic wrap or cover as soon as you see your seedlings.

INDOOR GARDENING

You should transplant your tomatoes once your seedlings are roughly an inch and a half tall. Choose the healthiest seedlings from each container, and move them into a larger container throughout the vegetative and fruiting stages of their life cycle. These young seedlings are going to need lots of light from the moment they poke out of the dirt, and this will continue throughout their life. They like it bright and warm, preferring to have between 18 to 24 hours of light. While this can make them an expensive plant when it comes to the electric bill, it also makes them an easy one to look after. You can just leave a light on rather than schedule an artificial day and night schedule for them.

You will want to use a liquid fertilizer with a high nitrogen content during this vegetative stage of your tomatoes. Continue providing them with 18 to 24 hours of light but pay attention to the temperature. Tomatoes are going to want their environment to be really warm, so keep the temperature between 75F and 80F. At night time you will want to drop the temperature to 70F. Regarding the soil, tomatoes enjoy a pH level between 6.0 and 6.8. Where tomatoes especially demand attention is their humidity level. Your plants are going to want a humidity level between 80% and 90%. This massive level is not going to be possible without a humidifier and some careful attention. During the night, this level drops down around 65% to 75%. The reason they want such a high level is due to the fact that tomatoes are primarily made of water. Tomato plants use water to keep the leaves and stem healthy and to produce the tomatoes themselves. They need so much water that the roots aren't able to keep up with the demand, and so they need to rely on transpiration to pull it out of the atmosphere.

Try to keep the humidity right in the middle, at 85%, or on the slightly lower end, around say 82%. This is because going above 90% can lead to the tomatoes suffocating. While they want plenty of water molecules in their environment, too many of these molecules will prevent the transpiration process from activating as it's supposed to. A humidity level that is too high leaves your plants at risk of flower drop, where blossoms fall off before maturing into fruit.

After the vegetative stage in the life cycle comes the flowering period. By keeping the light on for 18 to 24 hours a day, we are tricking the tomato plant into staying in the vegetative growth stage. Changing the lighting conditions of your tomatoes so that they begin by only getting 8 to 12 hours of light a day will trick them into thinking it's time to commence flowering. After you make this change in their lighting, you can expect to have fully grown tomatoes within the next 80 days. If you are planning to move your tomato plants to a larger container, then you will want to do this a few weeks before forcing them into flowering. This way, they have plenty of time to get used to their new home before they start to go through these changes. Once they have begun to flower, continue feeding them an NPK balanced fertilizer for the first two or three weeks. Then, following that stage, you are going to want to change to a fertilizer with less nitrogen and more potassium and phosphorus, as these nutrients are more valuable for the flowering and fruiting phases of a tomato's life.

INDOOR GARDENING

You are going to need to keep a close eye on your plants during this phase, particularly giving your attention to the flowers. You are going to need to start daily pollination from the point when the flowers first open up. The tomato flower has two primary parts involved in the pollination process. The first is the anthers (male) in the middle, and the second is the carpels (female), which are green pieces around the bud. The anthers of a plant primarily store their pollen on the outside, as this biological feature allows the pollen to be carried by the wind to pollinate the flowers. Tomatoes are a little more complicated, as their pollen is stored inside the anthers rather than on the outside. It is going to require vibration to get the pollen out of the anthers. In nature, this is achieved through the frequency of vibration that a honey bee buzzes. We can imitate this by using an electric toothbrush along the branches. Unlike strawberries or peaches, we aren't directly pollinating the flowers ourselves. Instead, what we do with tomatoes is vibrate them so that the pollen comes out and self-pollinates. This lack of control is why it is best to do this practice every day until the flowers turn into tomatoes. The other reason to do it so frequently is to produce more delicious tomatoes. The more pollen that manages to fertilize the plant, the more seeds there will be in the tomatoes themselves, and this means a much richer and tastier product. Once the tomatoes begin to grow, simply continue to look after the plant just as you have been doing, and harvest them when they are a bright and even red.

Cultivating Cucumbers

As with any plant, the first step is to decide what kind you are interested in growing. All sorts of cucumbers grow vines that like to climb all over what is around them. These don't necessarily require a trellis, but most growers want to train them to one to keep them orderly. Cucumbers are also known for having long taproots that dig deep into the soil. Varieties which forego this feature make for better plants when it comes to indoor gardening since there is only so far down the plant can dig into a container. A cucumber of the bush variety will have a much more contained growth, and that makes it a good fit for indoor gardeners. Once you have your seeds chosen, simply go ahead and plant them directly. Cucumber seeds have softer shells that don't require any extra work to start germinating. You can expect to see the seedlings poking out of the soil in about ten days.

Much like tomatoes, cucumbers prefer to have a source of continuous light. This extra light allows the cucumber seedlings to grow faster and more abundantly. If you are unable to provide them with continuous light, then simply light them for as long as you possibly can, with a minimum of eight hours of lighting a day. Transplant them into a larger container after they have been sticking out of the soil for a week or so. In terms of earth, cucumbers can grow in most potting mixtures, but they prefer loose soil with good drainage and plenty of organic plant matter (compost) to provide them with nutrition. They like to have a pH level between 6.0 and 7.0. A temperature between 65F and 75F during the day is ideal; just remember to drop that down to between 60F and 70F at night. In terms of humidity, cucumbers are rather unique in their needs. During the day, they like to have their humidity in the range of 60% to 70%. At night, they want a higher humidity level, somewhere in the range of 70% to 90%. While you can blast cucumbers with 24 hours of light while they are in the early stages of their growth, you will want to dial this back to 8 hours of light as they move towards their fruiting stage.

Cucumbers are very thirsty plants, as you might have guessed by their love of high humidity levels. As your cucumbers begin to fruit, they will require even more water. Use the finger test every day to ensure that the soil is moist. If you find that the top inch is dry, it's time to water them again immediately. Letting your cucumbers go thirsty is a recipe for disaster, so don't neglect this aspect of their care. You should also feed your cucumbers with a liquid fertilizer once every couple of weeks. An NPK balanced fertilizer is good, but what is extremely helpful to their wellbeing, is to provide them with a higher nitrogen supply, while still being mindful that the pH level stays between 6.0 and 7.0.

In keeping with the rest of the plants we've looked at throughout the book, when cucumbers flower, they have both male and female parts. There will be many more male flowers than female flowers. You can tell the female flowers apart because they will have tiny cucumbers growing behind them. To pollinate the females, you should remove a male flower from the plant and carefully peel back its petals as they store pollen on the inside just like tomatoes. With the petals peeled back, you can use the male flower like a brush. Simply run the male flower across the female flower. For the best possible results (aka the tastiest!), use a male flower from one cucumber plant to pollinate the females of another plant and vice versa. .

Continue to provide your cucumbers with plenty of water and nutrients while they fruit, and you will have fresh cucumbers in no time. From sprouting to harvesting often takes about sixty days. To harvest, simply pluck off the fully grown cucumbers by cutting the stem with your shears. Make your cut about three-quarters of an inch to an inch and a quarter from the top of the cucumber. Any cucumbers that are taking on a yellow color should be cut off and thrown out, as these unhealthy cucumbers will continue to grow and divert precious energy from the good ones.

Growing Edible Eggplants

Eggplants are originally from India, yet they have become a staple of dinner tables all across North America. While they can be hard to grow in your backyard, growing them indoors is a much easier experience and one that adds a nice variety to your indoor garden. As with any indoor garden, since space is an issue, it is always best to choose a variety of eggplant that isn't going to take up too much room. The little fingers, or fairy tale types, are delicious plants that don't need too much space. Starting with your small seed trays, fill them up with your potting soil and dig two small holes about a quarter-inch deep. Drop a seed or two into each of these and cover with soil. Remember not to pack the soil too tightly. Water the seeds immediately and then cover with a lid or plastic wrap. Keep these seeds

INDOOR GARDENING

at 75F with 12 to 14 hours of light per day. Remove the plastic wrap and use your spray bottle to mist the top of the soil on a daily basis. Use the finger test to see if the top inch is dry, and water when it is. Reapply the plastic wrap cover afterward. In one or two weeks, you will see seedlings sprouting out of the soil, at which point you can remove the plastic wrap or lids.

Judge which seedling is the stronger of the two and transplant this one into a larger container when it has grown to a height of roughly an inch. Eggplants like soil that drains quickly, with plenty of holes in the pot to allow for water to come out. Since they are originally from India, they enjoy drier conditions than many of the more traditional garden vegetables. Make sure there is plenty of compost in your potting soil mix to provide them with lots of nutrients. You will also want to spike a small trellis into the pot to help support the weight of the eggplant as it grows. Now that they have been transplanted, they should be comfortable in a slightly warmer environment, somewhere between 75F and 85F. Continue using the finger test to check the soil and water when the top inch is dry. You should also continue misting the plants every day. Eggplants like the humidity to be right in the middle, so aim to give them about 50% humidity. Feed them with an NPK balanced liquid fertilizer, and make sure you do this every week.

Wait for your eggplants to blossom and then use a brush to pollinate the flowers. Eggplants pretty much reproduce the same way that strawberries do, so go over each of the flowers at least twice to ensure you have done it comprehensively. You will see the eggplant itself begin to grow. These plants have a longer life cycle compared to the others we've looked at, so you can expect it to take upwards of 100 days before they are ready to harvest. You will know the time is right when the skin of the eggplant is a deep purple color with a glossy shine, almost like a fresh coat of metallic paint.

INDOOR GARDENING

Chapter Summary

- Indoor tomatoes should be a dwarf species, such as a cherry or plum tomato. Some varieties often grown indoors include pink ping pong, Siberia, micro tom, totem, red robin, or patio tomatoes.

- Tomatoes take between 50 to 90 days to grow from flowering to harvest. Chemical processes can speed this up, but the resulting tomatoes won't taste as good.

- You may want to add hydrated lime to your potting mix when it comes to tomatoes, as this will introduce more calcium. This element also helps prevent blossom end rot.

- Tomato seeds don't need to be prepared before you plant them. Simply plant the seeds, water them, cover the containers in plastic wrap, and wait for the seedlings to start poking through the soil. A temperature of 80F is perfect for germination. You can expect seedlings in one or two weeks.

- Transplant tomato seedlings when they are an inch and a half tall, choosing the healthiest of the seedlings to move. Throughout this period, the plants will want between 18 to 24 hours of light as they grow nice and large.

- Use a liquid fertilizer with lots of nitrogen during the vegetative stage. Keep the temperature between 75F and 80F, dropping the warmth

INDOOR GARDENING

down to 70F at night. Maintain a pH level between 6.0 and 6.8 with a humidity level between 80% and 90% during the day, and 65% to 75% at night. It is best to try to keep the humidity in the middle; too high or too low will damage the plants.

- Tomato plants need to be forced to flower when grown indoors. You can accomplish this by changing their lighting from between 18 to 24 hours to between 8 and 12 hours a day. You can expect to be eating your tomatoes 80 days from when you forced them to flower. Flowering tomatoes will want an NPK balanced fertilizer for the first couple weeks before switching to a fertilizer with less nitrogen and more potassium and phosphorus.

- As soon as the flowers begin to open up on your tomato plants, you are going to start pollinating them. In order to properly pollinate tomatoes, you will need to vibrate the flowers by using a tool such as an electric toothbrush. So long as you vibrate each flower, they will take care of the rest of the pollination process. Just make sure to do this every day until the tomatoes begin to grow; this will result in a tastier, meatier harvest.

- Cucumbers are known for having long taproots and growing lots of vines, so they will require a trellis and a deep container. Cucumbers of the bush variety will take up less space, making them ideal for indoor gardeners.

INDOOR GARDENING

- Cucumbers like to have light at all times. If you can't provide 24/7 light, then make sure you give them a minimum of 8 hours a day. Cucumbers also tend to want a pH level of between 6.0 and 7.0 and a temperature between 65F and 75F for the day and 60F and 70F at night. Their humidity level goes up at night, too, as they want between 60% and 70% during the day and a whopping 70% to 90% at night.

- Cucumbers require lots of water, so make sure to give them something to drink whenever the top inch of the soil is dry. Mix in a weekly treatment with a liquid fertilizer that is NPK balanced. Cucumbers also need lots of nitrogen, so you may consider feeding them a little extra as part of your fertilizer routine.

- Cucumbers need some help pollinating. Remove a male flower from the plant and peel back the petals to expose the pollen. This flower can now be used as a brush to put the pollen onto the female flowers directly. Cucumber plants benefit most by using the male of one plant to fertilize the females for another.

- You can expect to be eating your cucumbers within roughly sixty days or so after they first start to sprout.

- Eggplants don't need any extra work to plant, just drop a few seeds into a hole, and provide them with a temperature of 75F and 12 to 24 hours of light a day. You will want to mist them daily throughout this period as well.

- Eggplants require soil that drains quickly, but they can stand drier conditions than many of the other garden vegetables you will grow indoors. Provide a temperature between 75F and 85F as they grow, watering them only when the top inch is dry. However, you will still want to continue misting the plants on a daily basis. Use an NPK balanced fertilizer on a weekly basis.

- Use a brush to pollinate the flowers of the eggplant in the same manner that you would with strawberries. It will take upwards of 100 days before your eggplants are ready to be harvested, making them one of the slowest crops that you'll grow indoors.

In the next chapter, you will learn how to grow herbs like thyme, mint, or rosemary indoors. While herbs are often at the back of the queue in the minds of indoor gardeners, they can add some terrific flavors to your meals and take your cooking to the next level. They also grow very well indoors, with many growers beginning their exploration of gardening with herbs before moving onto vegetables or fruits.

CHAPTER SIX

PLANTING HEALTHY HERBS

While fruits and vegetables may be what most readily comes to mind when considering an indoor garden, you shouldn't overlook the value of cultivating your own herbs. Many gardeners first get into indoor gardening by starting a small herb garden. They're easy to care for and don't take up a lot of space. Of course, you can always scale up the size of a herb garden so that it takes up a lot of room, but, when compared to peach trees or eggplants, these little plants are downright tiny.

But they provide more than their fair share of flavor and aroma. While a herb garden won't put a full meal on your dinner table, it will make the food on that plate taste fantastic. In this chapter, we will look at growing a couple of the most common and versatile herbs. But before we do, let us first turn our attention towards why these herbs make for such a compelling addition to any indoor garden.

The Benefits of Herbs

Herbs are mostly thought of as a kind of spice, a plant that alters a dish to give the taste some extra depth. When you consider how many recipes call for mint, dill, basil, sage, rosemary, cilantro, or thyme, it is easy to see why herbs are so strongly associated with flavor. This reason alone is enough for many people to want to start their personal herb gardens; they are low maintenance, fun to grow, and mighty tasty. If this were the only property that these small plants possessed, it would still be well worth the trouble of cultivating them. But there is a whole world of health benefits that comes from adding herbs to your diet (and your garden). Looking at just a handful of these benefits will make it crystal clear how powerful these plants are. Remember that this is far from a comprehensive list, and there are even more benefits and more varieties of herbs than could conceivably fit in this book. They really are that impressive!

Sage is an earthy tasting herb that comes in two common forms, Salvia officinalis (plain) and Salvia lavandulaefolia (Spanish sage). A member of the mint family, small amounts of sage are used in quite a few dishes to give added zest to the natural flavor of the food. As little as one teaspoon of sage packs a great many vitamins and minerals, including 10% of the daily recommended vitamin K. It's also loaded with more than 160 different polyphenols which the body uses as antioxidants; some of these are believed to improve brain health, and are thought to lower an individual's risk of contracting cancer. Even if sage didn't do anything else, it would be an amazing little herb. But it's also been linked to reducing dental plaque and cavities, alleviating the symptoms of menopause, lowering blood sugar levels, and reducing LDL cholesterol. There are also studies showing that sage can be used in the treatment of diarrhea, improving the overall health of bones, and even reducing wrinkles and other signs of skin aging.

As mentioned earlier, sage is a member of the mint family. Perhaps the most well-known member of that family is peppermint, which is a staple ingredient of countless candies, teas, and extracts. The most common use of peppermint is to freshen your breath (that's why mints are offered after meals, and why it's also commonly used to flavor toothpaste), but this only scratches the surface of the benefits this aromatic herb offers. Another reason that peppermint is offered after a meal is due to the effect it has on the digestive system. It can relieve such unpleasant symptoms as indigestion, gas, and bloating, as it relaxes the muscles in the gastrointestinal tract, and has even been shown to reduce symptoms associated with IBS. Because of the effects it has on muscles, it's been used to treat tension headaches, and it has been linked to a reduction in headache pain when applied locally as an oil. Peppermint also has antiviral and antibacterial properties that help to open up your sinuses when they have been clogged due to colds. Peppermint has been linked to reduction in fatigue and to an improvement in energy levels. It seems to be effective in easing menstrual cramps, improving mental concentration, and helping with allergies related to seasonal conditions. Plus, there are studies showing that peppermint can reduce hunger pangs and therefore assist in weight loss. It's been used to promote restful sleep. It even appears to be good at killing off the harmful bacteria responsible for harmful infections such as E. coli or salmonella. So you can see, this aromatic herb has far more attributes than a pleasant taste.

Thyme is another of the mint family, which is arguably one of the most beneficial and wide-ranging families of plants on this planet outside of the papaveraceae group.

Often used to spice meals, there are actually more than 400 varieties of thyme. Their use dates back to the ancient Egyptians who used the plant as part of their embalming practices, and the ancient Greeks who burned it as a form of incense because of its attractive aroma. In regards to health benefits, thyme has been shown in animal studies to reduce the heart rate of rodents with high blood pressure, as well as to reduce the level of cholesterol in the same subjects. The use of thyme oil was shown to boost benign feelings in human subjects because of the active ingredient carvacrol. Carvacrol has a direct effect on the way that neurons in the brain function and regular use has been linked to an improvement in feelings of happiness and wellbeing. When the leaves of thyme are crushed to produce oil, the resulting juice can be taken orally to alleviate sore throats and to suppress coughing. The effect can also be achieved by adding thyme leaves to your tea; you can just pluck the leaves straight off your indoor plant. Not only does it help to reduce sore throats and coughs, regular use in tea or meals can help to strengthen your immune system in preventing colds in the first place. Thyme is a good source for vitamin C, copper, fiber, manganese, vitamin A, and iron, making this simple herb a super-healthy addition to your dinner. Beyond health benefits, thyme is often used as an ingredient in pesticides, and studies have shown that it even repels mosquitoes. Keeping thyme near your other plants can help to deter pests, though it is most productive in this manner when the leaves have been rubbed together or crushed to release their oil. Also, that same oil can be employed to help battle mold, since it has fungicidal properties that make it a useful ingredient in natural disinfectants and cleaners.

As you are probably starting to see a theme emerging here, let's only look at the benefits of one more herb. Far from just being a pretty name, rosemary is an aromatic herb that has been used extensively in traditional Hindu medicine. It is native to the Mediterranean and South America, but found its way into the North American market, and has become a staple of herb gardens all across the continent. It is part of the lamiaceae family that includes mint, basil, and oregano. Used to spice food or brew tea, this powerful little herb has a great many antioxidants that have been linked to protecting the body from inflammation damage and a decrease in the risk of cancer, heart disease, and type 2 diabetes. Rosemary also has anti-inflammatory properties because of its polyphenolic compounds. Other elements in rosemary have antimicrobial properties that enable the body to fight off deadly infections. This is one reason why traditional medicine has made use of it for centuries. Blood sugar levels have improved in individuals who use it, and research suggests it is beneficial in improving mood and memory. If you want to improve your memory and concentration, you can take it orally, but studies show that simply inhaling the aroma improves these areas as well. The link between rosemary and brain health doesn't stop there. Rosemary brewed into tea seems to have a positive effect in preventing brain cells from dying. Ongoing research suggests it may be beneficial in recovering from such traumatic brain injuries as strokes or reducing the effects of neurodegenerative diseases such as Alzheimer's. Rosemary has been linked to improving eye health and slowing age-related eye diseases, and both delaying and reducing the severity of cataracts. Along with all these terrific qualities, it's also beneficial in helping reduce the after-effects of a heart attack, reducing indigestion, and improving weight loss. Possibly, it may even improve hair growth; research has certainly shown it reduces hair *loss*, but there are more studies required to see if it promotes growth, though many people have claimed it does.

Looking at less than five herbs, we have seen that they have health benefits for nearly every area of the human body. Bear in mind: it should not be thought that the use of herbs removes the need for medical care - this would be a mistaken idea. Rather, the health benefits of these herbs should be thought of as supplemental to proper health care. We only looked at four herbs here, but there are more than 200,000 different subspecies within the designation of herb. This massive variety leaves a great deal of room for more benefits to be discovered through research. It also means there are more flavor combinations for your meals than could be listed in this book or even a hundred such books. In order to experience those, you're just going to have to start growing your own and experimenting with your dishes. So let's now turn our attention over to raising herbs as a part of our indoor garden.

Growing Thyme Indoors

In addition to the health benefits we explored above, thyme makes a wonderful addition to your salads, as a garnish on meat, or as an ingredient in your pasta sauces. As you will come to see with most herbs, thyme is very easy to grow, and many people have been successful in raising thyme plants just by letting them stand on a windowsill. The biggest trick to learn when it comes to growing herbs (and thyme is no different here), is figuring out how to pick it for use while keeping it alive so it can continue to produce.

The most common way that thyme is grown is through propagation. We can do this by taking cuttings from the tips of leaves and planting these, or it can be done by dividing a mature plant. To divide a mature plant, simply remove your thyme plant from its container, and carefully pull the root ball and the stems apart so that you now have two root balls rather than one. Replant the original ball in the same container and plant the new ball in a second container. With that simple move, you now have two thyme plants. If you want to grow from seed, then all you need to do is scatter thyme seeds in your chosen container, cover them with soil, water them, and then cover the container with plastic wrap. The bowl should be set in a warm location to wait for germination to take place. Despite being a soft-shelled seed, thyme plants can take anywhere from seven to eighty-four days to begin germinating. What this does mean is you really won't know if the seeds were viable or not until almost a hundred days after planting. This uncertainty dissuades many people from growing thyme from seed, especially when propagating is so simple and quick.

Thyme is often grown on windowsills because it prefers to have lots of bright light. It benefits from having direct sunlight, though, if it isn't feasible in your area, it can be compensated for by your grow lights. Growing thyme using electric lights can be a smart choice as they will let you raise this herb all-year round rather than seasonally. Thyme likes plenty of water but not all at once. You need to allow the soil to dry out before watering it again, as too much moisture will cause thyme to rot. Your best bet is to use the finger test to a depth of two inches, watering only when both inches are dry. Thyme has a resistance to the harmful effects of drought, so it is better for it to be too dry than for it to be too moist. Because of how harmful moisture is, thyme should be planted in a lightweight soil with plenty of pockets for air to move through and quick drainage. Likewise, thyme does not require any extra humidity as this also promotes rot; you should grow thyme away from your indoor fruits and vegetables in an area that has plenty of airflow. Fertilize thyme on a weekly or bi-weekly basis with an NPK balanced liquid fertilizer applied to the soil rather than the plant.

Raising Rosemary

As rosemary comes from the Mediterranean, its environmental preferences reflect that climate. It's a herb that can tolerate droughts and craves plenty of direct sunlight. Much like thyme, rosemary is more often than not purchased as an already growing plant, rather than in seed form. Choosing to grow from seed is as simple a procedure as thyme; merely plant them and wait for them to grow. Be aware they also take a long time to grow from seed to dinner-ready. It is far easier to purchase rosemary as a plant, and then take leaf tip cuttings to propagate a new plant.

INDOOR GARDENING

You will notice that we didn't bother talking about repotting thyme. That's because it's a small plant, and the only time it ever needs to be repotted is if you purchased it from a store and decided you wanted to move it to a different container. Rosemary, on the other hand, can grow up to four feet in height and takes up much more space than thyme. If you want to keep rosemary at a smaller size, then you need to repot it during the spring and prune the size of the root down by a third before planting it back into a container of the same size. If you do want it to keep growing larger, simply wait until spring and transplant it into a bigger container.

Rosemary likes lots of sunlight, between 8 to 14 hours a day. The rule of thumb with most of the Mediterranean herbs is that the more light you can provide them, the healthier they will be. Just as with thyme, rosemary will begin to rot if it has to deal with too much moisture. Use the finger test to make sure that the soil is dry before watering. This is a case where overwatering will kill the plant, but underwatering will hardly affect it at all. Since it loves bright light and direct sunlight, this means it wants plenty of heat. Keep the temperature between 50F and upwards of 80F, sometimes even higher. Just remember that the hotter the temperature is, the more airflow will be required to keep it healthy. Plant rosemary in a soil that drains quickly, and use a liquid fertilizer weekly, applying to the earth rather than directly on to the plant itself.

INDOOR GARDENING

While rosemary has plenty of issues that may affect it, such as too much moisture causing it to rot, the biggest problem that growers face is preventing powdery mildew from taking hold. This unpleasant fungal disease is prone to strike plants that are overly moist, under-lit, or lacking in proper air circulation. You can tell powdery mildew from its white, powder-like appearance. It looks almost as if someone has sprinkled flour over the leaves of your plant. Treating this mildew can be a real pain. Since rosemary is a herb, it is primarily grown with the intention of being ingested by humans. Therefore, if it should acquire a disease, you don't want to treat the problem with harmful chemicals that will make you sick. If you spot any powdery mildew on your plant, you should immediately remove all of the parts that have been infected and dispose of them outdoors. Next, reduce how much you are watering the plant and ensure that it is getting enough sun and circulation. Neem oil should be used on your plant regularly, long before any signs of the mildew. After all, prevention is always better than cure. If you have been applying neem oil and your rosemary has still been infected, then increase the regularity of use and supplement with baking soda as a natural remedy.

Maintaining Mint

INDOOR GARDENING

Mint is a particularly forgiving plant, able to grow just about anywhere you may want to put it. Of course, it does have its preferences, but as far as plants go, it is remarkably flexible in a way that makes it a good choice for first-time gardeners setting up an indoor operation. But the versatility that it shows in growing is vastly outperformed by the versatility it demonstrates when it comes to consumption. Mint leaves can be used to flavor teas or relishes, or add a delicious layer of flavor to yogurt or ice cream. It is used to garnish meat dishes, or it can be tossed in a salad, and there are many drinks, both alcoholic and non-alcoholic, that use it as a core ingredient. When you combine this adaptability with the health benefits mint has, it is easy to see why everyone would benefit from adding a bit of mint to their garden.

As far as containers go, mint will need to be housed in one that has drainage holes at the bottom to help it dry out properly. Unlike rosemary or thyme, mint enjoys more moisture, but too much is still going to impact its health negatively. If you need to make a choice between a wide container or a deep one, go with the wide one, as mint grows and spreads in a lateral fashion rather than a vertical one. In fact, mint spreads so quickly that if you were to plant it in an outdoor garden, then you would have to be extra vigilant in ensuring it doesn't choke out the other plants in the bed. We avoid this tricky problem by growing it indoors.

Mint likes to have a pH level between 6.0 and 7.0, and it grows best when the potting mixture has plenty of sand mixed in to promote quick drainage. However, like many herbs, the pH level is far less important to mint than it is to fruits or vegetables. Herbs have a tendency to be resilient to problems involving the richness of their soil. That said, if the pH level is going to be off, then it is better to be too low rather than too high as an overly high pH level can promote extremely troublesome fungal infections. For the best results, replace the soil once a year. Mint will suck out all of the nutrients quickly, and adding compost will only maintain the soil's longevity up to a point. It is also strongly recommended that you add a top layer of mulch to create a defense against harmful bacteria and that you reduce the frequency of watering.

The most common way of growing a new mint plant is to take a clipping of the stem from slightly above a leaf.

INDOOR GARDENING

Take this clipping and place it into a glass of clean water, or into a perlite and vermiculite mixture that has been moistened ahead of time. Ensure that each cutting is a few inches in length and that it has some new growth. After a week or two, you will notice roots beginning to form at the bottom of the clipping, at which point you can then repot it. Other ways to grow mint are to divide them by removing the plant from its container, splitting the root ball into two, and then planting each ball into a separate bowl. To grow mint from seeds, you will need to scatter seeds throughout a container, frequently mist the soil, and wait for upwards of three months for germination to take place. Mint seedlings are especially fragile, so great care must be taken when handling them or even when watering them. As a rule of thumb, growing from seed has the lowest success rate while dividing has the highest. Dividing is the quickest way to get new plants up, followed close behind by cuttings. In the time it takes to grow a seed, you could have started new plants from cuttings three times over.

Mint enjoys the sun, but it likes to have partial shading rather than direct light. That said, it likes to have light throughout the entire day. If you need to provide an electric lighting setup for your mint plants, then you are going to want to get the lights very close to the plant itself. Expect to give mint between 8 to 10 hours of light in a day. When it comes to watering, mint wants to be kept moist, so the best way to check if it is time to water is to do a reduced version of the finger test and simply check the top of the soil. If it is dry to the touch, then it is time to water. Mint also enjoys a higher humidity than the other herbs we looked at, with around 70% being ideal. If you cannot provide your mint with humidity at this level, then regular misting will help to provide it with enough moisture in the atmosphere. Mint doesn't particularly need much fertilizing, although a bi-weekly treatment with an NPK balanced solution applied to the soil can help. Be mindful of how much you are fertilizing mint and the smell and taste of it. Too much fertilizer will reduce the flavor.

While mint is quite easy to look after, it does have one extra step that others don't. Mint will bend towards the source of light, giving it an unhealthy appearance, almost as if it were wilting. While this isn't in any way unhealthy, it is unseemly. Rotate the container twice a week to prevent this lopsided look.

Chapter Summary

- While herbs are primarily added to dishes and consumed for their flavors, they have a vast range of health benefits that make them a wonderful addition to any home garden.

- Sage is jam-packed full of vitamins and minerals, with more than 160 polyphenols. It has been linked to reductions in cases of cancer, and improvement in brain health, as well as dental health, reduction of menopause symptoms, lower blood sugar, and lower levels of LDL cholesterol. Sage is also used in treating diarrhea and improving bone and skin health.

- Peppermint freshens your breath and promotes digestive health. It is also used in treating headaches and has both antiviral and antibacterial properties. Peppermint has been linked to improved brain health and concentration, reduced menstrual cramps, improvements in sleep, and it helps to kill off harmful bacteria.

- Thyme reduces blood pressure and harmful cholesterol, boosts mood and mental wellbeing, alleviates sore throats and coughing, is filled with lots of nutrients, and can even be used to repel pests that want to turn your garden into a snack bar.

- Rosemary helps repair inflammation damage, reduces the risk of cancer, type 2 diabetes, and

INDOOR GARDENING

heart disease. It has been shown to help with blood pressure, mood and memory function, and even help prevent brain cells from dying. Rosemary has been linked to other areas of health: these include the eyes, the hair, and recovering from heart attacks.

- There are more than 200,000 different subspecies of herbs, meaning you have an endless variety to experiment with for reasons of health and flavor.

- Thyme is easiest to grow through propagation, cutting off clippings to create new plants, or splitting the root ball to produce two identical plants. Growing from seeds takes months and has a much lower success rate.

- Thyme likes to have lots of light and plenty of water, but the soil should be left to dry completely between waterings as too much will cause rot. Keep thyme in an area with low humidity and earth that will promote fast drainage.

- Rosemary likes hot areas, lots of sun, and dry periods between watering. Like thyme, it is best to create new plants through propagation instead of growing from seed. Rosemary grows several feet in length, so clipping the roots once a year should be done to keep it at a consistent size.

- Rosemary shouldn't be exposed to too much moisture, as this promotes both rot and the growth of powdery mildew. Provide plenty of airflow to help reduce this, and remove any infected leaves as soon as you notice them. Treatment with neem oil and baking soda together can help to defeat an infection if caught early.

- Mint likes lots of drainage in its soil and lots of moisture. Check the top of the soil to see if it is dry, watering when it is. A daily misting will help to ensure that mint gets the 70% humidity it desires. Plenty of nutrients in the soil is fine for mint, as it likes a pH level between 6.0 and 7.0. It is better to go below 6.0 than it is to go over 7.0, as mint can withstand lower pH levels far better than it can higher.

- Keep mint in partial shade for 8 to 10 hours, providing it with an NPK balanced fertilizer once every few weeks. Too much fertilizer will drain away the flavor, making the taste test a good way to see if you need to reduce your fertilizing schedule. Rotate mint twice a week to prevent it from growing lopsided.

In the next chapter, you will learn the most common mistakes that new growers make. We will consider faults such as failing to keep the growing space clean or ignoring warning signs of nutrient burn, infection, or poor environmental conditions. By becoming aware of such pitfalls, you can be sure you'll avoid these costly mistakes and keep your garden healthy and beautiful.

CHAPTER SEVEN

COMMON MISTAKES AND HOW TO AVOID THEM

When it comes to gardening, there are a great many errors that growers are prone to make when they start out. In fact, truth to tell, there are many gardeners who continue to make mistakes despite having acquired years of experience. The most common reason that mistakes are made is ignorance. Some people simply think that if they can raise carrots, then they can raise lettuce, or if they can grow an orange tree, then they understand how to take care of mint. This attitude ignores the subtle (and not so subtle) differences between plants, and simply reduces a vast topic into too rigid a formula. When this happens, dead plants and poor harvests are prone to follow.

While the chances are that you will make mistakes of your own during the early stages of creating your indoor fruit, vegetable, or herb garden, this chapter aims to make you aware of the most common mistakes that new

INDOOR GARDENING

growers are likely to make. By being aware of these mistakes, you reduce your level of ignorance, and you increase your chances of avoiding them yourself. Now, this doesn't mean that you will, by default, avoid these mistakes simply because you read this chapter. But it does mean that you have the knowledge necessary to avoid them so long as you act on it. In the world of growing, much as with life in general, we are required to act on our knowledge if we want to see the best results.

Not Doing Your Research

We've looked at a handful of plants throughout this book, and, while some of them share similarities (such as thyme and rosemary), they all have notable differences in how much light, water, fertilizer, space, and humidity they want, as well as which nutrients they like best, and what pH level they require to stay healthy. If there can be this much of a difference between the small handful that we were able to look at, then you can only imagine how much variety there is across the plant kingdom. Not only that, but keep in mind that different subspecies of plants often have their own preferences that, while similar to each other, can show a great deal of variation. All this adds up to the fact that you should never make an assumption about the needs of a plant.

Instead, do your research on your plants. If you have access to the internet, then a quick Google search will reveal link after link about how to raise whatever kind of fruit, vegetable, or herb you are considering. If you aren't very technologically savvy, then you should consider stopping in at your local gardening center and asking them for advice. The chances are good that you were going to get your seeds from them anyway, so why not pick their brains first to find out everything you need to know. Questions you should consider asking are: How often should I water this plant? What type of fertilizer do they need and how often do they need it? Does it take long to germinate? How long does it take to grow? When can I expect it to start fruiting? How much light does it want? Does it prefer direct sunlight or partial shade? What temperature should it be kept at? How much humidity does it require? What pH level will it need? Is there anything I should know about pollinating it by hand? Are there any health risks I should be aware of?

Asking questions and doing your research should be the very first step you take when considering growing something that is new to you. Before you even look up the price of seeds or seedlings, ask all the questions you need answering, whether or not you are capable of providing an ideal environment for this type of plant. Being prepared with information will save you money as you can avoid those that aren't a good fit, and you will also spare yourself the disappointment of watching a new plant wilt and die.

Growing Too Much At Once

When they're beginning, many people have big, grand plans for their indoor gardens. They're going to have lettuce and tomatoes, carrots and eggplants, a peach tree, some rosemary, and a bunch of mint. In theory, this sounds amazing. Who wouldn't want to have that much delicious food at their fingertips? But in practice, this is often a recipe for disaster.

The first issue that many people are going to run into by expanding too fast is the fact that things aren't growing as they thought. Just because you plant a seed, doesn't mean it is going to grow. It can be particularly discouraging for new gardeners when it happens once, but consider when it happens to several plants all at the same time. Furthermore, even if they do germinate, each plant is going to grow at a different rate, and this means that you will need to balance the needs of a number of different plants that are all at various stages of development. Pay special attention to the use of that word "balance." Gardening takes up your time and attention; you need to watch your plants to get a sense of how they are doing, and then adjust their care accordingly. While you might think that this will be quick and easy, many new gardeners are completely shocked at just how long this can take.

When you are starting, begin small and then expand as you become more comfortable with looking after a garden. While I would suggest starting with a single plant, many will find this to be too small to make it worth their time. If you need more, allow yourself two or three plants but limit yourself to this. Pick plants that have similar care routines and environmental requirements so that you can worry about building one environment, rather than fine-tuning several. Take these plants through to harvest before you add any more. That way, you know what is required for each step in the care process. Start slow, and add more as your skill and understanding increases. Approach it with a sensible attitude. Looked at this way, becoming proficient at gardening is not that different from any other skill.

Planting Seeds Too Close Together

When you are first putting seeds (or even seedlings) into a container, it will seem like there is an abundance of space. After all, seeds are super-tiny, and so you can put a whole whack of them in a container without it feeling like they are crowding each other out. While this is true at these early stages of growth, you will quickly come to regret this decision when your plants start to grow, and you realize that they have no space at all. But why is this a bad thing, necessarily?

First off, while you will notice the lack of space on top of the soil, it is really what is happening under the soil that is damaging your plants the most. Their roots are going to start to get tangled and fight to find their own space while they grow, and this is going to cause a number of issues that negatively affect their overall health. Those same roots are going to have to compete with each other for nutrients, and this means that all of your plants are going to be far less healthy when compared to those that get all the nutrients they need without a struggle. The struggle to fight for nutrients wastes energy, energy which would be better utilized in promoting growth. Stunted plants are one such result from being planted too close together.

Another factor to bear in mind is that pests and disease can much more easily spread from plant to plant when they are too close together. Moreover, they have more places to hide; it is much harder to see all the nooks and crannies of your plants when they obscure each other. Therefore it's evident that planting too close together creates more difficulties with pests and diseases and smaller harvests of less tasty food.

Not Checking for Pests or Cleaning for Disease

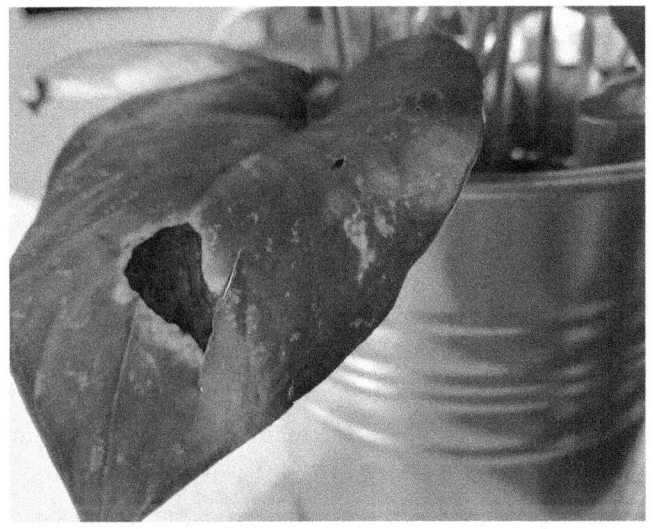

Speaking of pests - have you been checking for them? If not, then how do you know that your plants are still healthy? Just because you don't see pests when you look at your plants doesn't mean that they might not already be feeding off your plants. There are many telltale signs of infection such as discoloration in leaves, bumps or holes in the leaves, or leaves that have begun to wilt for no discernible reason. The longer an infestation takes hold, the more damage your plants will sustain, and they can only take so much before they give up and die.

You want to ensure your plants are free of infestation or infection; the simplest precaution is to check them daily. This takes up time, that resource many new growers discount when they decide to grow too many plants. While many pests can be detected on sight, there are more than a few that either hide or are invisible to the naked eye. If you see pests, you need to start treating your plants immediately. But you should also do spot tests on a daily basis to see if any such parasites are hiding. Use your rake to check the soil at the roots, as many pests lay eggs in the soil; the offspring of these eggs will, given the chance, chew away at the stem. Next, take a piece of paper towel or toilet paper, and wipe the bottoms of the leaves. If the paper comes away with streaks of blood, then there are pests you are going to have to deal with. There are many methods of dealing with pests, but you should do your research before embarking on any of them. Since fruits, vegetables, and herbs are all plants that we grow with the intention of eating, it's crucial to ensure that whatever pesticide or solution you use to treat your plants is not going to harm the food you eat.

While you are making it a habit to check for pests, you should also keep your eyes open for signs of disease. White powdery mildew, molds, discoloration, wilting branches, rotting fruit - all of these are signs that your plants have caught a disease. The first step in tackling most sicknesses is to cut away any infected parts and immediately dispose of them outdoors. Apply treatments to your plants after ensuring those treatments aren't harmful to humans.

There are several key steps you should take to avoid disease in the first place,. Apply neem oil on a weekly basis, even if there are no signs of infestation or infection. This is a preventative measure so that you won't have to deal with these annoyances. Also, keep a close eye on how much water and light the plants are getting to ensure that they aren't getting too little or too much. Next, check the pH level of the soil to make sure that they have enough nutrients, as too few can leave them sickly, and too many can cause nutrient burn. Finally, though just as importantly, make sure that dead plant matter is removed from the area. The compost that is used in the soil is fine, but leaves or branches that have fallen off the plants and are rotting in the general area are quite harmful. This rotting plant matter, when it isn't being used as part of a properly planned feeding system, can introduce harmful bacteria to your growing area. Always make sure you remove any dead or fallen plant matter from the growing area and wash your hands first before you start handling your plants.

INDOOR GARDENING

Chapter Summary

- The most significant cause of mistakes that new indoor gardeners encounter usually originates from either ignorance or simplistic assumption.

- Every plant is different, and this means that every plant has different needs, though some elements of those needs may be similar to others. Even within a particular kind of plant, the various subspecies may have vastly different environmental needs compared to each other.

- There are a great many questions that you should ask when you are first considering planting a type of plant that you haven't worked with before. These can often be answered by asking these questions of Google or through approaching a knowledgeable employee at your local gardening center.

- Researching should be the first step you take before starting with any new plants.

- Beginners often aim big and plant all sorts of different plants with the intention of enjoying them on their dinner plate in the near future. What they overlook is the difficulty associated with maintaining multiple types of plants simultaneously, and how much time and energy it takes to look after a full garden.

- It is always smarter to start with one to three plants and bring them from seed to harvest,

INDOOR GARDENING

before branching out and increasing the size of your growing operation. A modest beginning will give you a sense of how much effort it takes to properly grow your fruits, vegetables, or herbs.

- When you have your plants too close together, their roots begin to fight each other for nutrients. This wastes energy that would be better employed in growing into healthy adult plants. Planting too close together will leave you with small, sickly plants.

- Planting too close together also makes it easier for pests and diseases to spread from one plant to the next. They won't need to travel as far, and there are more parts of the plants that are obscured from the scrutiny of the gardener.

- Signs like discoloration, bumps, or holes in your leaves are telltale signs of either infestation or infection. Many pests can be tricky to spot if you aren't specifically looking for them and, if left untreated, they can kill your plants.

- Check the soil and the bottom of your leaves to see if there are any pests hiding where you can't see them. Make it a habit to check daily.

- Infection can spread quickly through a plant, and any infected leaves or branches should be cut off and disposed of outdoors. Dead plant matter around the growing space can introduce harmful bacteria into the environment. You should

INDOOR GARDENING

always clean up and tidy your growing area every day, washing your hands afterward before you touch your plants again.

FINAL WORDS

Creating an indoor garden is no more difficult than growing one outdoors. Indeed, the level of control that we have over an indoor environment makes it easier in many ways. Rain, drought, chill, or snow no longer mean death for your plants, and through the use of electric lights, you are able to provide enough "sunlight" to ensure your plants stay healthy and happy.

In order to properly grow plants indoors, you are going to need to invest more money into ensuring you have a proper environment for them. Nonetheless, a lot of this money is used in the earliest parts of the setup, such as purchasing grow lights, fans, or humidifiers. Once you have made the investment in this gear, you will be able to reuse it again and again for crop after crop. Viewed that way, the investment becomes easier to justify. Not only that but if you decide that indoor gardening isn't for you, then you can resell this equipment to make back some of your money. Just remember to start small when you begin; otherwise, the cost of your investment, and the time you need to commit will be much higher.

As we deal with issues like global warming and changing environments, indoor gardening will continue to grow in popularity. In the future, it seems likely that a substantial proportion of our foods will be grown and raised inside, rather than outside. What this means is that the skills and knowledge you have gained from this book are going to become more relevant to daily life, and more in demand in the coming years. Starting your indoor garden today will give you the practical experience you need to teach others how to start theirs. Not only is indoor gardening a great choice to be able to enjoy organically-grown fruits and vegetables from the comfort of your home, but it's also an investment in you and your family's future.

We have only been able to cover a small selection of the plants that you can grow indoors. You shouldn't feel limited to sticking to those that we have discussed throughout the book. Instead, you should take the lessons we've gone over here, and apply them to the fruits, vegetables, and herbs that most interest you. Just remember to do your research to ensure that you can provide the right environment for your plants, be they blueberries, basil, pumpkins, or anything else. Each plant is unique and you should respect it as such. With this attitude and a little attention, you will be able to grow anything your heart desires.

So what are you waiting for? Put this book down and go get your hands dirty tending to your own indoor fruit, vegetable, and herb garde